William Payne

A Plymouth Experience

David Japes

ACKNOWLEDGEMENTS

I am grateful to the staffs of the Public Record Offices at Chancery Lane and Kew and particularly to Miss G.L. Beech for providing material and references. The following London Galleries and local Fine Art dealers generously provided photographs of drawings by Payne and other artists: The Leger Galleries, Spink and sons, Thomas Agnew and sons, John Mitchell and son, J. Collins and son of Bideford, W.E. Fox Smith of the Barbican, Plymouth and Heather Newman of Painswick.

I received the utmost courtesy and help from the following reference libraries and local history departments: The Guildhall Reference Library, The Westminster Reference Library, Buckingham Palace Road, the Greenwich Local History Library, the Marylebone Reference Library, the Holborn Reference Library, Theobalds Road, the West Devon Record Office at Coxside Plymouth, the Westcountry Studies Library, Exeter and the East Sussex Records Library at Lewes.

The Watercolour Department at Christies and its then Director, Anthony Browne, gave me much valuable help and made available their extensive file of Payne illustrations.

My debt to the Royal Albert Memorial Museum, its Director, Mrs. Hilary McGowan, and staff, is very great. Above all, I must put on record my gratitude to Jane Baker, Fine Art Curator at the Royal Albert Memorial Museum. Not only did she take up this project with enthusiasm but, with dedicated hard work, saw it through to its ultimate completion. As a result of her efforts a Payne exhibition, for which this account will form the catalogue, has again become feasible after a lapse of more than half a century. The burden that has fallen on the Museum was discharged with much good humour and expertise by a willing band of permanent staff and helpers, notably Rachel Sommerville, Chris Reed and Frank Gent. Dr Michael Pidgley was also generous with his time and sound advice.

I am grateful to the City Museum and Art Gallery, Plymouth and its Fine Art Curator, Maureen Attrill for their encouragement and the loan of several important drawings by Payne. I am equally grateful to all the other owners who have kindly lent pictures to the exhibition.

To my father my debt is very great. He undertook much of the research at Kew while I pursued enquires at Chancery Lane. His encouragement, financial support, and expertise in the field of genealogy were decisive factors in bringing the project to fruition.

The original script was typed without any complaint about my spidery scrawl by Katy Bickle of Cullompton and, at home, by my wife. The final typescript and the design was organised by Vikki Venables with great expertise and despatch.

The author and organisers of the Payne exhibition are grateful to the Leger Galleries Ltd. of London for generous financial support towards the cost of the publication.

Dedicated to My Father
with grateful thanks.

Published to coincide with the exhibition, William Payne (1760-1830) – A Plymouth Experience, held at The Royal Albert Memorial Museum, Exeter. September 15th – November 28th, 1992.

Set in Garamond 10pt and printed in Great Britain by Brightsea Press, Clyst Honiton, Exeter, Devon.

ISBN: 1–85522–183–7.

CONTENTS

INTRODUCTION

William Payne, the inventor of Payne's grey, a colour still used today, was a prolific watercolourist. He has always had his devotees. It is all the more surprising then, that very little was known about him. What was known can be stated briefly. He first started exhibiting at the Society of Artists of Great Britain in 1776 from an address in Park Street, Grosvenor Square. In the 1780's he was working at Dock, Plymouth, and from there sent pictures, mostly of Devon and Cornwall, to the Royal Academy and to the Society with whom he had first exhibited. By 1790 he had returned to London, where he became the most fashionable drawing master of the day. But despite this success, his contemporaries failed to record either his parentage or the place and date of his birth. When and where he died were equally unknown. Details of his life were sketchy, and he last exhibited in 1830. Various reasons were suggested for his presence at Dock and for his removal to London. The sources are contradictory, and none of them bears close scrutiny.

William Payne's life spans the period which saw the rise of the English Watercolour School. At the beginning watercolourists were the poor relations in the English artistic scene. However, Paul and Thomas Sandby, most of whose work was in watercolour, were influential founder members of the Royal Academy, and benefited from Royal patronage.[1] Watercolourists proved the ideal companions for young noblemen on the Grand Tour. Some recorded antiquities for the expeditions of the learned societies, and others provided a valuable record of sights seen on far-ranging embassies. By the 1780's, as foreign travel became difficult, and finally impossible, because of the war with France, artists discovered the scenery of their own country. The watercolourists, in particular, were influenced by the theories of the picturesque and the sublime developed by writers like Burke and Gilpin.[2] Many of them were amateurs,

for drawing masters had by this time proliferated, as skill in watercolour became a desirable social accomplishment. Connoisseurs began to collect drawings, and one of them, Dr Thomas Monro, invited aspiring young artists to his London home, and gave them drawings by Hearne and J.R. Cozens to copy.[3] Turner and Girtin were two of these young artists, but there were others who were influential later in the founding of the Old Watercolour Society. By the end of the 19th century, when histories of the Watercolour School came to be written, some of the earlier artists were only dimly remembered. Their work was disregarded because fashions had changed, and some, like Towne, dropped from sight, only to be rediscovered in this century. Although he never disappeared completely, Payne was one of the casualties.

Everything had started well for the young artist. Some of the works that he had sent from Plymouth to the Royal Academy were engraved by Middiman and reached a wider audience.[4] A view of Plympton was lavishly praised by Sir Joshua Reynolds, the President of the Royal Academy, either because the drawing reminded him of his own birthplace, or because he assumed that Payne was a fellow Devonian. As a result, Payne found a ready sale for his pictures. But, as a successful drawing master he did not need to exhibit, and the resulting lacuna—a nineteen year gap before he exhibited anywhere again—was damaging. Farington only makes a passing reference to him in his Diary as the teacher of John Glover.[5] By the 1820's he was almost forgotten, and although W.H. Pyne acknowledged his success as a tutor to the sons and daughters of the nobility in the mansions of St James' Square, Grosvenor Square, York Place and Portland Place, he accused Payne of initiating an epoch of degeneracy in Art, dismissing his teaching methods as a wilful perversion of taste.[6]

It is hardly surprising, when later writers, like the Redgraves, surveyed a century of British art, that neither they, nor Roget, who followed their account in his "History of the Old Watercolour Society", could discover much about Payne.[7] Payne had in fact joined the Old Watercolour

Society in 1809 but resigned in uncertain circumstances, four years later. If Payne had remained in it, Roget would have had more to go on. Instead, all three writers engaged in speculation and it is from this stage on that misconceptions and falsehoods about Payne began to accumulate. The Redgraves stated categorically that Payne was a Devonian who left Plymouth in 1790 to seek fame and fortune in London. A similar suggestion was made by Algernon Graves, a well-known writer on art, who, when a correspondence on Payne was started by J. How in the journal "Notes and Queries" in 1880, replied that Payne was a Plymothian and a self-taught artist, though he admitted that Payne's first-known address posed problems. The correspondence attracted its usual share of eccentrics, one of whom asked if Payne had any connections with Matthew Payne, a Coventry musician. This was duly noted by Roget and found its way into his book.

A serious attempt to rehabilitate Payne and to discover more about him was made in this century. Unfortunately, it only added to the confusion, though this was not the author's fault. In January, 1922, Basil Long, Keeper of Prints and Drawings at the Victoria and Albert Museum, wrote the first monograph on Payne. He had previously contacted Mr R.F. Franklin, Secretary to the Admiral Superintendent at Devonport Dockyard, for information on Payne and was told that in 1780 there were two Paynes working at Dock— Ralph, who was Clerk to the Survey, and William, Second Assistant to the Master Shipwright. Long assumed, not unnaturally, that he had found the reason for Payne's presence at Dock, and he suggested that the two Paynes were related. It is not clear if Long visited Plymouth, though he included a circular drawing from the Plymouth Museum's collection among his illustrations. If he had examined an inscription on the reverse, he would have seen that it provided a clue to the real reason for Payne's presence in Plymouth, which was at variance with the one suggested. Basil Long failed to unearth any more information. As a result, the lack of a precise chronology prevented him from placing the different phases of Payne's artistic output in context.

Amongst later writers, Colonel M.H. Grant, in a "Dictionary of English Landscape Painters" (1926), reminded readers of Payne's quality as an artist in oils as well as watercolour, but unearthed little that was new, apart from the existence of a son of William Payne, a W.R. Payne, exhibiting in London from 1802. The compiler of the catalogue for the Payne exhibition at the City Museum and Art Gallery, Plymouth in 1937, incorporated Long's new information, but disregarded his caveats on Payne's origins. Both Iolo Williams, in his "Early English Watercolours" (1948), and Martin Hardie, in his "Water-colour Painting in Britain" (1968), are more cautious. They refer to Payne as an engineer rather than a shipwright, perhaps recalling a statement by Ruskin in 1849, and were more concerned with evaluating Payne as an artist. Iolo Williams correctly identified a Sandby influence in some of Payne's early work, and Martin Hardie, in comparing Payne with Francis Nicholson, concluded that Payne was the better artist. But even Hardie was not averse to some speculation. He gives some date between 1755 and 1760 as a likely one for Payne's birth, and makes use of another diatribe from Pyne, written in 1831, and its uses of past tenses, to back up his belief that Payne had died in 1830.[8]

I had long ago decided that biographical details were essential in understanding William Payne's art. Firstly he seems to be working in three distinct styles, all inter-related, it is true, but with a clear break in 1790. Since this coincided with the traditional date of his move from Plymouth to London, it seemed important that an attempt should be made to answer these questions. Was William Payne a native of Devon? Was he self-taught and, if not, who were his teachers? Why does he give a London address in 1776, alternative Plymouth and London addresses in 1786, '88 and '89 and only London addresses thereafter?[9] The 1937 Plymouth catalogue says that the reason for the 1776 address must forever remain a mystery, but it was a mystery that I felt should be solved.

It is not the purpose of this account to chart the stages

which led to this answer. Suffice it to say that the date of Payne's death was relatively easy to establish. The rest emerged more or less in reverse order.

What, then, of the tradition? Some of it was correct, though often misleading in its presentation. Much of it, however, was wrong.

1. THE FAMILY BACKGROUND AND THE EARLY YEARS

William Payne was born on March 4th, 1760, the son of William Payne and his wife Eleanor. William senior was a hop and coal merchant residing at Westminster and William was baptised at St. James's Church (now St. James, Piccadilly) on March 20th, 1760. William and Eleanor had married in the same church on June 9th, 1758, by licence from the Archbishop of Canterbury.[10] The place of residence is not given in the licence, except that it was in Westminster—and indeed, William senior's name does not appear at this stage in the Westminster Rate Books—but his age is recorded as "twenty eight and upwards" on May 11th, 1758 (he was actually twenty eight and nearly two months) and Eleanor's as over thirty. William appears to have been their only child, to judge from the parish baptismal records (a fact confirmed by his father's Will).

William's father came from Burwash in East Sussex, close to the Kent border. Two of his four sisters were still living there in 1794 (the other two had migrated to Hawkhurst and Rye) and one, Anne, on her marriage in 1757, is recorded as a "spinster of the parish of Burwash". William senior was baptised there on March 22nd, 1730, the son of yet another William (who was alive in 1757 and signed as a witness at his daughter's wedding) and his wife Ann.[11]

By the 1750's William senior had left Burwash for London. At this stage he was probably only selling hops and would initially have made for the Southwark area where the hop merchants and their factors were congregated. One third of all the hops in England were grown in Kent and the bags, or pockets, as they were called, from Kent, Sussex and Surrey arrived by road from the oast houses for the market which had been established in the 18th century in the Borough after its removal from Little Eastcheap. From there the hops were purchased from the factors by the merchants and distributed to the numerous inns at Southwark, or despatched across the river. William Payne's business would have been lucrative, for by the last three decades of the century an average of two million barrels of beer were brewed in the London area annually and for this six to eight million pounds of hops were needed.[12] Beer drinking had by then overtaken gin consumption and a quart of beer at 3d could be afforded by journeymen and apprentices. The elder Payne's removal to Westminster may have coincided with his decision to add coal to his interests.

The connection between hops and coal is not obvious at first sight, but it made sense in mid-18th century London. Although there were over twenty brewers in London at this time, of which the largest was Samuel Whitbread's at Chiswell Street, St. Luke's, many of the inns and alehouses, particularly those concentrated on the Middlesex side of the Thames, brewed their own beer. The landlords of the inns stretching eastward from Holborn to the Tower supplied lodgings to the large, vagrant Irish community, most of whom followed the occupation of coal-heaver: in return for board and lodging their services were hired out to the coal merchants. The place where the coal merchants gathered, was at this time situated in the Fish Market at Billingsgate immediately opposite Southwark, though much of the business was still carried out, as in the early years of the century, in the public houses near Billingsgate, and the districts surrounding the Tower. It made sense, therefore, for William Payne senior to combine the selling of hops and coal.[13] For this, barges would be needed and added to, as his prosperity increased. By the 1770's his efforts were rewarded and it was probably then that he acquired two houses at Greenwich which are mentioned later in his will. Indeed, he may have had a wharf there, for a Mr Payne hired Madox's wharf at Greenwich from 1769 to 1773.[14] It has to be remembered that coal was an almost totally sea-borne trade in the 18th century: the coal was transferred from the Newcastle colliers to the barges at various points in the Thames estuary. The number of barges was in excess of one thousand, accounting for a third of all the vessels on the river.

It is important to establish the social status of William Payne senior in view of the plans he had for his son. In the early part of the century Daniel Defoe had classified the English into seven classes:
The great who live profusely
The rich, who live very plentifully
The middle sort, who live well
The working trades who labour hard but feel no want
The country people who fare indifferently
The poor, that fare hard
The miserable, that really pinch and suffer want

In the London of the 1770's the only change that had taken place in these groupings (omitting, of course, the fifth class) was the fusion of the third and fourth groups. Indeed, some tradesmen could match the income, if not the social status, of the second group. Patrick Colquhoun, writing in 1805, gives the annual income of the third group as £700-£1500. Such are the people who appear in the rate books of fashionable London with the suffix esquire, or if not, were classed as gentlemen. Above them were the landed gentry, with large estates, from the minor aristocracy upwards. It is likely that, by the 1770's, William Payne's hop and coal business was bringing in an income in excess of £500 annually, a large income at a time when the wage of a labourer or lower paid craftsman was 12s 0d per week. Strangely enough, coal heavers could earn as much as 10s 0d a day for irregular work. Not content with this, they tended to riot frequently in the 1780's.[15]

By 1774, William Payne senior had prospered enough to move to Park Street (fig. 1) and his name appears for the first time in the Westminster Rate Books.[16] In 1775 his name appears too, for the first time, in the London directories, recording him as a hop and coal merchant of Park Street, Grosvenor Square.[17] It is impossible to say whether William Payne senior was a coal merchant, providing coal primarily to retailers from his barges, or whether he retailed it as well. The Park Street address would suggest the latter.[18]

The move to Park Street was shrewdly timed, for the Grosvenor Estate was nearing completion and had become the most fashionable area of London. Indeed, the history of London in the 18th century shows a gradual migration westwards by the wealthy from the once favoured areas such as the piazza of Covent Garden, St. James's and Soho Square. The Hanover Square and Cavendish Square projects led the way in the 1720's, Grosvenor Square was completed by 1753, and most of the surrounding streets by the 1760's. Only the areas north of Oxford Street and around Bedford Square remained to be exploited but a start was made here too in the 1770's.

We must be cautious in reading too much into an address like Park Street. The figures in the rents column of the rates books, even in these areas, were often quite small—for Park Street North, where William Payne senior resided, the rents amounted to £16 per annum. It has been pointed out that the rent column figure was not strictly a rent but the equivalent of a rateable value.[19]

The real reason for living there was the proximity of the wealthy in the more fashionable streets and squares. In Park Street there were only three titled residents, one doctor, a general and two esquires. The rest, like William Payne senior, are merely recorded by their names.[20] In the whole Grosvenor Estate, tradesmen accounted for 9% of the total, but in Park Street the proportion was much higher. Fifty out of the one hundred and nineteen houses were occupied by tradesmen. It was, in fact, one of the streets in which the fashionable shops were situated, as well as a centre of the coachbuilding trade. William Payne senior was the only coal merchant that I have been able to trace in Park Street, though there were about twelve in the Grosvenor Estate.

Park Street North had been virtually completed by 1770, except for three sites. In 1778, the last three houses were designed and built by John Crunden on the lower or western side of Park Street North and one of them belonged to Mrs Fitzherbert.[21] It was in this house that the Prince Regent, later George IV, secretly married Mrs Fitzherbert in 1785. His visits there, prior to that, were equally surreptitious—through the back door via Tyburn Lane. When William Payne moved to Park Street, the executions at Tyburn were still continuing and drawing large crowds. They ceased in 1783 after representations from residents in Park Street and other streets close to the route to the gallows.

Although the houses in Park Street have long since disappeared, the "Survey of London" described the average 18th century house there as "small for the most part, three bays wide, with a narrow entrance passage and staircase, two moderate rooms on each floor and closet wings at the rear." They are described as "suitable for a single gentleman or a small genteel family".[22] One of the houses survived into the 1920's, No. 64, an inn known as the White Bear, and this is illustrated in the "Survey of London". It is difficult to speculate which house William Payne senior occupied as the rate books do not give the numbers, but assuming that Park Street was a working address and that there would have to be storage space for some coal (the bulk would have been held at the nearest wharf or on his barges), the most likely houses are No. 60 on the lower side or No. 40 on the upper, both of which have independent rear access. Whether William's father rented the house, or purchased the lease, is not known.

An additional reason for the move was, in all probability, the talent that the fourteen year old William was beginning to display in drawing. It was also becoming clear that he would probably not follow his father into the hop and coal business. Before discussing the most likely place in which William would have received instruction in draughtsmanship, we should examine the teaching methods commonly employed in the 18th century. At drawing schools like Shipley's in The Strand, the exercises largely consisted of drawing from plaster casts of Greek and Roman antiquities. Other drawing masters set their students the task of copying engravings after 17th century artists. According to Farington's Diary, there had been an increase in the numbers of such drawing masters since the 1750's, the most important of whom was Paul Sandby.[23] The engravings most commonly used were the prints of Vivares or Earlom after Gaspard, Salvator Rosa and Claude Lorrain. A typical example from Richard Earlom's mezzotints of Claude's "Liber Veritatis", is the *Landscape with Narcissus*. In this are all the features of imaginative landscape in a classical setting as understood by 18th century artists: on the left, a mass of trees and rocks, and to the right, a single tree enclosing a pool, leading the eye to the central point of the composition, a castle clinging to the edge of a rock. Beyond is a vista of a curving coastline and distant hills. The figures reclining in the foreground and a herdsman crossing a bridge in the middle distance add scale to the view (fig. 2). In the British Museum there is a copy by Payne of a similar scene after F.E. Weirotter. Both the original and Payne's copy are in sepia (figs. 3, & 4). The British Museum also contains a student work by Paul Sandby of a much earlier date, "Book of Figures with the Prospect of Edinburgh Castle" (1746-7), which has, on the title page, an ink sketch showing an artist drawing from ancient sculpture and inside, a series of copies from engravings by Abraham Bloemart in addition to the Prospects of Edinburgh and other Forts, which are in an altogether different mood. Sandby had received his training in the Drawing Room at The Tower of London and such factual drawings are in the topographical tradition which extends from foreign artists resident in England like Wenceslaus Hollar through to artists such as Francis Place. The significance of this tradition in Payne's work will become clear later.

In 1776, William Payne, by that time sixteen, sent a drawing to the Society of Artists of Great Britain. Its title, *A Landscape,* suggests an imaginative work of the kind described above, rather than a topographical view. The Society of Artists had held exhibitions since 1760 and by 1766 was generally attracting artists less well known than the exhibitors at the Royal Academy, which Paul Sandby had helped to set up in 1768. However, some artists of eminence, among them the Sandbys, continued to support the society.

The 17th exhibition opened on 18th April, 1776, a little later than the usual date, and the committee who judged Payne's work as worthy of inclusion consisted of John Hamilton Mortimer, Sawrey Gilpin, John Dixon, Francis Wheatley, John Smart and William Marlow. With the exception of Dixon (an architectural draughtsman), these were established artists, mostly born in the 1740's and consisting of figure and cattle painters (Mortimer, Gilpin), a landscape and genre painter (Wheatley), a topographer (Marlow) and a miniaturist (Smart). Possibly, in his early figure drawing, Payne was influenced by Wheatley, for it is sometimes reminiscent of him, though at other times closer to artists of the Sandby School with whom a more definite connection can be established.

William Payne did not exhibit again at the Society of Artists until 1790, nor anywhere else until 1786. The reason for this must now be given. He was receiving precise training in draughtsmanship by 1776, for in April 1778 he was appointed as a draughtsman, fifth class, at the Board of Ordnance Drawing Room in the Tower.[24] The records for the Board are now kept in the Public Record Office at Kew, but there is a secondary list of Ordnance employees and of the Drawing Office personnel in the Tower, included in the contemporary Court and City Register, produced every January from 1758. There are discrepancies between the two lists and these have to be sorted out, when they occur, by referring to the Board records, in particular the Quarterly Lists. These state the salaries of Ordnance Officers, giving dates for their employment and the places they served in. Luckily for us, a separate list of trainee fourth and fifth class draughtsman for 1780 and 1781 has survived in the Ordnance records attached to drawings of maps and forts. This gives the ages of the draughtsmen on 1st September 1780 and 1st January 1781, as well as their years and months of service in the Tower, and covers the period when William Payne was starting his career. In this we are told (wrongly, as it turns out, by some few months; there are a number of discrepancies in these lists; see Appendix III) that his age was twenty one on 1st September and still 21 on 1st January, his years of service being two years five months and two years nine months respectively.[25] Some of the draughtsmen in Payne's time were still boys: two were twelve, one thirteen and three fourteen. The two youngest had entered the Drawing Room at the age of eleven. It is doubtful, in view of this, that Payne was trained as a boy at the Tower, and his early training in draughtsmanship and drawing must have taken place elsewhere. It is possible, though this cannot be proved, that he had taken lessons with Paul Sandby, whose house at 4, St George's Road, Bayswater was certainly within walking distance, across Hyde Park, from the Park Street address. However, intensive training began for Payne when he was eighteen, in 1778, at the Tower, under the three main instructors whose names are appended to the reports for 1780 and 1781 (see Appendix III).

Something must now be said about the Board itself in the 18th century. The Ordnance Board was set up before the end of the 17th century to look after the lands, depots and forts required for the defence of the realm and to supply arms and equipment to the Army and Navy. It maintained Engineering Stations (the dockyards), powder mills and laboratories (Fareham, Waltham Abbey), the Royal Observatory at Greenwich, and at the Tower of London it oversaw arms manufacture, and the copying of maps and plans, maintaining two outside areas for mapping operations at Portsmouth and Plymouth. Abroad, the ancillary establishments consisted of a chain of depots and stations in the staging posts of an expanding empire. It worked in conjunction with the Royal Military Academy at Woolwich which trained Artillery Officers and Engineers. The Tower was the nucleus of all these operations and the draughtsmen in the 18th century were civilians, independent of the military establishment, wearing blue uniforms which distinguished them from the red-coated officers of the Army. In the Drawing Room, young boys were taken as "cadets" and instructed chiefly by draughtsmen and mathematical masters in the draughting and copying of fortifications, plans and military topography.[26]

The requirements laid down in 1683 for the Chief Engineer serve as a model for what was expected of an engineering draughtsman in the Tower in Payne's time:

To be well skilled in all the parts of mathematics, more particularly Stereometry, Altemetry, Geodoesia. To take distance, heights, depths, surveys of land, measures of solid bodies, and to cut any part of ground in a proportion given... and to be perfect in Architecture, Civil and Military... to draw and design the situation of any place, in their due prospects, uprights and perspective... to keep perfect draughts of the Fortifications, Forts and Fortresses of our Kingdom, their situation figure and profile... To make plots or models of all manner of Fortifications, both Forts and Camps, commanded by Us to be erected for our Service.

This, of course, tells us little about the teaching means employed to achieve this end, but a clue is provided by the 1780 and 1781 records already referred to. These, as we have seen, set out a list of all the draughtsmen in the Tower and, apart from their ages, years of service, rates of pay and conduct, there are three columns giving their proficiency in Plan Drawing, in Mathematics and in Perspective. There were therefore three main elements of training for Draughtsmanship. The Mathematics was always reported on more fully in a series of separate reports, and these have survived as well. William Payne's performance here in Geometry, Algebra and Trigonometry fluctuated considerably in 1779. Usually moderate, and only once good (in December), he had a bad patch in July, August and September, his performance was "indifferent" in proficiency and twice he was referred to in the column dealing with application as "idle". His attendance, usually punctilious, was affected perhaps by illness, as the last column suggests, and he was absent without leave twice. He seems to have got over this bad patch, however, although his position was usually seventh or eighth out of a class of twenty.[27] His reports on Drawing and Perspective were always good and he was called "a good draughtsman". What was involved in plan drawing and perspective can be seen from the examples of the pupils' work appended to the lists. They were set the task of copying maps or plans of forts held in the Tower records. For example, there is a copy of a survey of 1750 of the road between Blairgowrie and Braemar, presumably part of the Survey of the Highlands on which Paul Sandby served, and amongst the elevation of forts there is one in Jamaica and a plan of a proposed gateway originally drawn in 1765 at Annapolis Royal, later home of the United States Naval Academy. One draughtsman, W. Allen, aged fifteen, had been set the task of drawing three pages of squares, twenty eight by seventeen per page, with diagonal lines of intersection. Clearly, this was the first type of exercise set them, before they moved on to maps and plans.[28]

The teaching of perspective would not have been confined, however, to the copying of earlier plans. Here we can make an inference from the teaching of the Woolwich Cadets in Paul Sandby's time. In 1768, Sandby became Chief Drawing Master at Woolwich, though the Board of Ordnance continued to pay his salary there (the amount from the beginning was £150 per annum and not £100 as most previous accounts state), and drawing was taught there as follows: "Landscapes, with Indian ink; large and more difficult landscapes, coloured; landscapes, coloured from nature; perspective, applied to buildings, fortifications, etc."[29] This was for the Senior Cadets, for whom Sandby was responsible (perspective was left to his assistant), and we must assume that he was merely repeating what he had been taught in the Tower which, according to tradition, he joined in 1747 at the age of sixteen, becoming briefly, by 1768, Chief Drawing Master.

Who then were Payne's teachers of Drawing and Perspective? The reports of 1780-81 are signed by George Haines, the Chief Draughtsman at the Tower, for Plan Drawing, and by Henry Gilder for Perspective. Henry Gilder was, from 1778 on, the Chief Drawing Master. Unusually, he was appointed from outside the ranks of the Tower Draughtsmen, at the age of twenty eight. A protégé and servant of Thomas Sandby, his assistant at Windsor, and an artist working very much in the Sandby tradition, he appears in the Tower list during one of Thomas Sandby's frequent absences (fig. 5). Thomas Sandby's career at the Board of Ordnance, intermittent though it was, extended from 1743 to 1796. He seems to have remained on the payroll even when his name does not occur in the Court and City Register, and both the quarterly lists and the 1780-81 report refer to him with the words "His Majesty" or "Attends His Majesty"—all of which is in accord with what we know of his career. We can speculate that Thomas Sandby's influence at the Board was considerable, and all the more so in view of his Royal connections. We are told by Farington in his Diary that King George III intended to give him a knighthood, when one was vacant, but he could not be found.[30] From Haines, Payne would have learnt the precise draughtsmanship required in Ordnance work, but Gilder was presumably responsible for the crisp and neat drawing which is seen in Payne's early watercolours, and which is his main inheritance from the Sandby tradition. Gilder, too, was a topographical artist with a firm grasp of architectural details and his work is like Payne's in its tonality (fig. 6).

Very few of the draughtsmen in the Tower go on to achieve distinction as watercolourists, but those who do seem to be working in the Sandby tradition. One of the draughtsmen in 1774 was James Miller who perhaps may be identified as the topographer well-known for his views of London in the latter part of the 18th century. Another, a contemporary of William Payne's, is George Bulteel Fisher, later Sir George, who was to serve with distinction as a Royal Engineer in the Peninsular Wars.

By William Payne's time, possibly because of the wars with France, the cadets and draughtsmen were instructed in French. There were also teachers of classics, and of fencing. There was a separate model maker. Although the social status of the draughtsmen was not the same as that of army cadets, the accomplishments they were required to possess were similar. Indeed, in 1774, one cadet, Robert Beatson, became a gentleman cadet after a mere thirteen days in the Drawing Room.[31] Payne's salary as a fifth class draughtsman was two shillings a day and his promotion was quite rapid. By 28th February 1783 he was a draughtsman, second class.

It is interesting to note that by the 1780's there were fifty two draughtsmen working in the Tower, a fourfold increase over the number in the 1750's.[32] This increase is partly explained by the Board's policy, in these years, of seconding Tower draughtsmen to Engineer Officers who were engaged in various projects. It is in this context that we can see the significance of the Sandby tuition—hitherto not sufficiently appreciated—and its role in the defence of the realm. For in Payne's time we have draughtsmen, trained by a protégé of Thomas Sandby, serving under officers who had acquired the rudiments of draughtsmanship at Woolwich under Thomas' brother, Paul. To make their secondment more effective, the Tower cadets put their training to practical use in an exacting apprenticeship of gun-drill, surveying and mapping, followed by further river and harbour surveys. During 1780 and 1781, William Payne is recorded as being "with Captain Page", firstly on his own and then, in 1781, with Robert Sturt. This Captain Page was Thomas, later Sir Thomas Hyde Page (1746-1821) of the Royal Engineers.

His career is well enough documented to reconstruct Payne's movements during these years and, indeed, to the end of 1782. Receiving an invalid pension as a result of wounds received at the battle of Bunkers Hill in North America, Page was appointed by Lord Townshend, Master General of the Board of Ordnance, as "Engineer of the Coast District". As a drainage expert, he was concerned with the supply of fresh water to dockyards and garrisons. At the dates given above he was concerned with the south east coastal areas, where William Payne would have joined him, and in 1782 at Sheerness where Page sunk an experimental well—with initially disastrous results—in the quicksands of the estuary. No doubt Payne and Sturt were responsible for mapping the area and drawing the well to Page's design.

Despite representations in Parliament about the cost, "not a well", it was said, "for fresh water, but a sink for the money of the public", he proceeded with his plan a second time with more success at Fort Townshend, receiving a knighthood the following year.[33]

William Payne remained with Thomas Hyde Page until the project was completed. However, there were other areas, apart from Sheerness, which were engaging the Board's attention. The 1780's were a critical period for Britain in the wars with France and the defence of coastal areas and dockyards was a matter of concern. While Payne was with Captain Page in 1780, two draughtsmen, Robert Sturt and Frederick Groves, were sent to Plymouth to assist Colonel Dixon of the Royal Engineers. There, the primary concern was the defence of Plymouth Dock itself and not the water supply, though the latter was a matter of friction between Plymouth and Dock. The first pair of draughtsmen were replaced by George Beck and R. Dickinson in 1781. By the end of 1782, it was clear that the extensive nature of the work demanded a more permanent presence. Dickinson was replaced, and William Payne and Robert Sturt were sent by the Board to join George Beck at Plymouth Dock. There is every indication that Payne was profoundly affected by the experience.

2.   PLYMOUTH DOCK

As we can now see from the preceding account, William Payne was not at Plymouth in 1780, nor was he the second assistant to the Master Shipwright. The lists in the Court and City Register (which also records employees of the Royal Dockyards) suggest that in 1780 there were only the Master Shipwright and a Second Master Shipwright, and it is not until later that more than two names are given.[34] In 1780 the Second Shipwright was W. Pollard and it seems that Basil Long's informant misled him. Ralph Payne's name as Clerk of the Survey does appear between 1778 and 1787 but he was clearly no relation of William's. It has to be remembered that Payne is a common name, not merely in Devon, but elsewhere, and no less than three William Paynes were married in Stoke Damerel Church between 1784 and 1789. One of those worked as a sawyer in the Dockyard. To add to the confusion there was another William Payne serving at the time in the Tower of London as Office Keeper to the Treasurer.[35]

Payne's presence in Plymouth was, as I have said, brought about as a direct result of the worsening situation in the wars with France. In 1778 the war had become international when a treaty of alliance was signed between the French and the rebel American Colonists. In 1779 Spain, followed by the Dutch, entered the war at a time when the British Fleet had been allowed to run down to pay back six million pounds of the national debt. It was not only the Fleet that was in less than admirable state. The defences of Plymouth, too, were in poor condition. To add to Plymouth's problems, at Millbay and in the hulks in the harbour, there were half-starved prisoners of war, American and French. Refugees and wounded soldiers were herded together in the Transport Ships. The inhabitants of Plymouth and Dock, always inclined to radicalism—it was the age of secular and religious radicalism—sided with the Colonists, descendants of men who had left for the New

World from the Mayflower Steps in Cattewater one hundred and fifty years before. Plymouth was awash with suspicion and rumours of plots. In this atmosphere of mistrust, one incident turned into broad farce. A spy in the pay of the French, a "Count Parades", though he was probably a pastry cook's son, obtained the plans of the Dockyard, and the fortifications of Plymouth by bribing his way into the Citadel and the Docks. Discovering that the defences of Plymouth were virtually non-existent, he took his information to France, returned with a French emissary, Berthois, was promptly arrested, escaped, and returned to France with an idea in his head for capturing Plymouth. The French authorities took up the plan with enthusiasm and instead of sending a force of four thousand suggested by Parades, despatched thirty thousand and an armada.[36] Contemporary sources should be allowed to take up the story:

1779—Thomas Blyth Darracott, Mayor. On the 15th August, Hardy was cruising in the soundings when French and Spaniards appeared off Plymouth; and some French frigates anchoring in Cawsand Bay captured a number of coasting vessels. On the 16th the Ardent, 64, fell in with the enemy's fleet, and, mistaking it for the British, was surrounded and captured within sight of Plymouth. The fleet consisted of 60 or 70 ships of the line, with a "cloud" of frigates, sloops, fire-ships, etc.

Fortunately for Plymouth, the French admirals did not believe Parades' information about the state of Plymouth's defences. They broke off the engagement and returned to Brest. The whole episode was turned into a drama which played to packed houses in London with words and music by Dibdin. There is one scene in which the Landlord of an inn on the Barbican asks a newly arrived customer:

"What's the news, sir? How many sail of the line now?"

"A hundred sail of the line, sir, and two thousand transports; the whole beach covered with

French troops as thick as fleas; a bridge of boats begun that's to reach from Plymouth to France, and we shall all be killed in less than an hour!".

The trauma of this event is also well summed up by the laconic enquiry of the Commissioner of the Dockyard to the Admiralty: "Shall I burn His Majesty's dockyard, or wait until the French Admiral comes in and does it?"

It was against this background that it was decided to put the defences of Plymouth in order, and to undertake an extension of the Dockyard which would match the first extension of 1725. William Payne was sent to Plymouth under a warrant dated September 1782 which set aside £512 for the year 1783 as salaries for those "employed in copying, contracting, draughts at the Drawing Room in the Tower", [37] and it is at this point that we read in the records for the first time: "At Plymouth—William Payne, 92 days at 3s. 6d. a day" (£16 2s. 0d. a quarter).[38]

Such salaries were paid to Ordnance employees on a quarterly basis and both they and, for that matter, the Dockyard Officials and workers had to wait for a boat carrying their money to arrive. This boat was despatched from below London Bridge and sailed to Plymouth each quarter. It is likely, therefore, that transport to and from Plymouth for Payne and the other Ordnance employees was arranged on this vessel and not overland by coach. For the next five years, his name and that of Robert Sturt appear with the addition of "at Plymouth" and often with the title of "Engineer". A comparison of the rates of pay for the Board's draughtsmen show that 3s. 6d. a day was one of the higher rates, and it underlines the importance of the work that he was doing.

His job was to record the profile of the existing, new and reconstructed forts at Plymouth, designed to protect not merely the Dockyard but the approaches of the Sound, and the entrances to the Hamoaze and Cattewater (see figs. 7,8 & 9). The work continued during the uneasy peace that followed the Treaty of Versailles. Surviving records suggest that Payne was concerned with individual defences, while Sturt produced more generalised maps of the area.

By 1783, the Plymouth end of the defences, and, in particular, the entrance to Sutton Pool and the Cattewater, presented less of a problem. The Citadel itself with cannon both on and below it, was impregnable, and there were batteries under Mount Batten and at the foot of Teat's Hill. (fig.7)[39]

The protection of Dock was causing greater concern. The town of Dock, which contained military barracks and Government House, was surrounded by a high wall, and from the landward side, at least, despite an earlier scare, appeared secure (fig.8). But there were areas outside the wall, including the Naval Hospital, and the Long Room Barracks, which were situated near Stonehouse. These relied for protection on the batteries situated out in the Sound on St Nicholas' Island, and on the shore, at Eastern and Western King. [40]

The Western King battery was also vital for the protection of the Hamoaze and the approaches to Dock. Opposite it, on the Cornish side, were blockhouses at Cremyll and at Mount Edgcumbe. The latter was one of the earliest forts in the area, described by Carew in his "Survey of Cornwall". The Western King battery needed strengthening, but the pressing need in the 1780's was the reconstruction of the Mount Wise fortification in Dock itself.

By the time of Payne's arrival the work had been started. Not only were the defences on Mount Wise strengthened but a battery was established below it.[41] Both Mount Wise and Western King became permanent redoubts, and there were two further redoubts at Stonehouse and Mount Pleasant (fig.9).

Plymouth, by 1783, had become the front line of the nation's defence now that the western squadron was of greater importance, and this was in marked contrast to the situation some nine years earlier, when a report had concluded that Plymouth "could never be the rendezvous for great fleets in time of war, for the want of safe and spacious roadsteads before the Harbour."[42] Despite the lack of a breakwater, which was not built for many years, all this had to change, and within the Dockyard, to emphasise its importance, a new unroofed dock was begun, to accommodate ships with masts, including, it was hoped, captured French vessels.

However, the Dockyard was still vulnerable to attack from another quarter. Above Mount Edgcumbe were the Heights of Maker, where the church tower acted as a signal station to the fort on Mount Wise. Colonel Dixon, the engineer responsible, with the help of one thousand Cornish miners, for the reconstruction of the Mount Wise fortification, had concluded that the defence of Maker Heights was an urgent priority. A series of redoubts was planned on Maker Heights on land purchased from the Earl of Mount Edgcumbe and the Rt. Hon. R. P. Carew.

William Payne was given the task of mapping the area and drawing the plans for its fortification. This map turns out to be his only surviving work, so far traced, for the Board of Ordnance.[43] The inscription on the central part of the map refers to a plan for five bastions or redoubts built to protect a pentagonal fort which had been designed by the Duke of Richmond. This reads:

Plan of works projected for the Defence of Maker Heights near Plymouth, but which are meant to be examined on the ground by a Committee of Engineers before they are executed. All the works are intended to have a whole Revetment and Counterscape in Masonry. The Main work is to have sufficient casemattes, magazines and store houses, bomb proof, and a barracks, and each of the detached works is to have a small magazine and casemattes bomb proof.

The date given is 4th April, 1783 and the inscription is signed Richmond, Master General—denoting the fact that the Duke of Richmond was the Master General of Ordnance—and a copy was made for the Chief Draughtsman at the Tower, Thomas Yeakell. North of the redoubts, Payne mapped out Millbrook Creek, and to the south, Cawsand Bay, over which he drew a profile of the five bastions. A futher inscription reads:

A Survey of the Heights of Maker, with a chain of detached Bastions, including two projects for a main fort, the one an irregular pentagon by his Grace the Duke of Richmond, the other a regular pentagon by Lieutenant Col. Dixon.

At the bottom right hand corner appears: "George Beck, Surveyor, drawn by William Payne."

The colouring is simple, greenish blue for the water of Cawsand Bay and Millbrook Creek, and yellow for the large fort. The central area, interestingly enough, is in washes, some strengthened, of the colour that has come to be known as Payne's grey—a compound of Prussian blue, lake and yellow ochre (figs. 10 & 11).

Although some of the survey work undertaken by Payne and his colleagues was not implemented, because of long parliamentary wrangles, the construction of the redoubts on Maker Heights proceeded. Two of them, numbers four and five, were built in accordance with the specifications indicated on Payne's map, and guns were moved up from Cawsand Bay. By the end of Payne's time in Plymouth these redoubts were ready to receive the additional cannon ordered for them.

No doubt Payne mapped other fortifications as well, for surviving watercolours depict coastal sites which possessed forts and batteries, such as Seaton, Port Wrinkle, and Wembury.

William Payne's tour of duty in Plymouth ran from March 1783 to 30th September 1788.[44] At that point he seems to have left the Board's service until the end of 1790. Possibly he was given leave of absence. At any rate, he was then pursuing a separate career as an artist and presumably having some success in selling his drawings. He first exhibited as a fully fledged artist in 1786 and in that year and the three following he was able to send pictures to the Royal Academy during his periodic visits to London, as indicated by the London addresses in Tottenham Court Road and Soho Square. In 1786 and 1787, most of the pictures are of

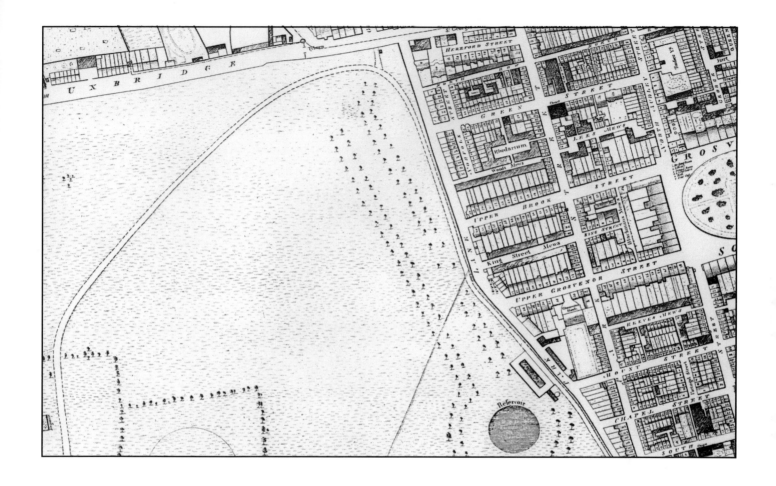

Fig. No.1

Map of the Grosvenor Estate, Mayfair, with Park Street c. 1785

Courtesy of the Westminster Reference Library, Buckingham Palace Road, London.

Fig. No.3
Franz E. Weirotter (1739-1771).
Classical Landscape.
Sepia wash; 4½ x 7¼ inches.

Private Collection.

Fig. No.4
William Payne.
Landscape after F.E. Weirotter.
Sepia wash.

Courtesy of the Trustees of the British Museum.

Fig. No.5
Paul Sandby (1731-1809).
Portrait of Henry Gilder. (1750-1789).
Black and red chalk; 7¾ x 4½ inches; Inscribed "Henry Gilder, servant to Thos. Sandby, drew remarkably."

As the text of this book makes clear, Thomas Sandby was probably influential in obtaining Henry Gilder the post of Chief Drawing Master to the Board of Ordnance Drawing Room in the Tower. Doubtless this was a reward for his loyal service to Sandby as well as a recognition of Gilder's talent as a draughtsman, which was mentioned in the Board's reports on his work (see Appendix III). The presumptive date of Gilder's birth, unknown before, is based on Board of Ordnance records, which also give 1789 as the year of his death.

Fig. No.6
Henry Gilder (1750-1789).
Ruins of Cowling (Cooling) Castle near Stroud, Kent c.1779.
Pen, ink and watercolour; 8 x 11⅞ inches.

Gilder, formerly servant to Thomas Sandby (see Fig. 5) became Payne's drawing master at the Board of Ordnance and the similarity between Gilder's style and that of Payne's early drawings can be seen in the use of the pen, the figure drawing, and the treatment of the foliage and sky. Note too the contrast between dark shadows in the foreground and sunlight beyond. Gilder's pen line is fussier than Payne's but its use on the railings to the right of the tower entrance should be compared with that on the pier in Payne's view of Wembury House (46).

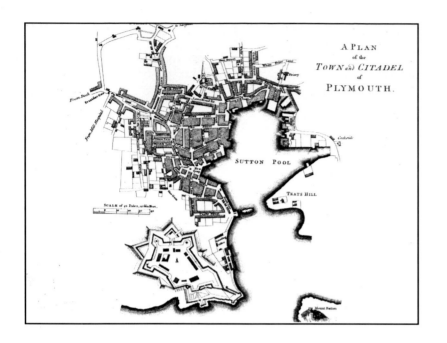

Fig. No. 7

Map of Plymouth (c.1765-75) by Donne.

Private Collection.

Fig. No. 8

Map of Dock (c.1765-75) by Donne.

Private Collection.

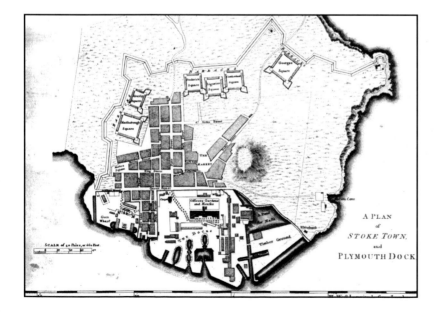

Key to Sturt's Map. (Opposite)

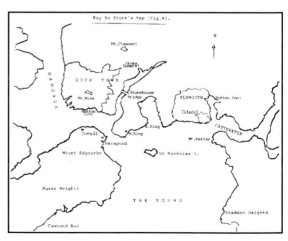

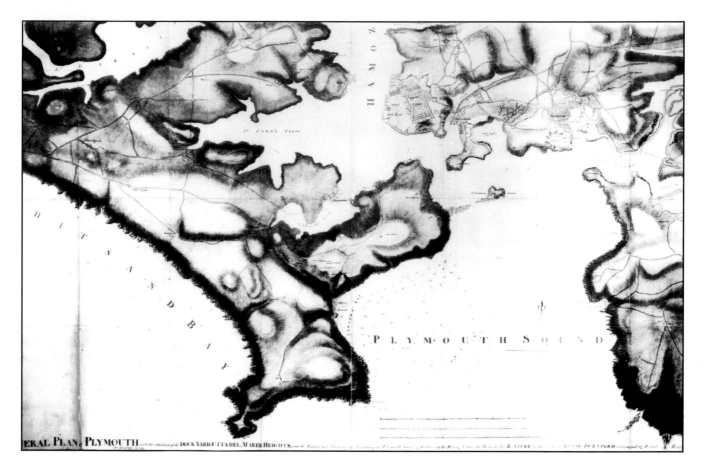

Fig. No.9

Robert Sturt. **General Plan of Plymouth with the situation of the Dock Yard, Citadel, Maker Heights, and the Environs, showing the soundings in Plymouth Sound and distances of the Rising Grounds, 1788.**

Robert Sturt, who was the witness at Payne's marriage to Jane Goodridge in 1785 and godfather to Payne's eldest son, William Robert, joined the Board of Ordnance in 1779, and was superannuated on full salary in 1802. A talented maker of maps, he produced at least four maps of Plymouth between 1783 and 1793, staying in the vicinity of Dock for a longer period than Payne.

Fig. No.10

Survey of Maker Heights with a project for a main fort with detached bastions.
Plan and Sections 2ft. 6.9in. x 5ft. 1.8in..
Surveyed by G. Beck and drawn by W. Payne, 1783.

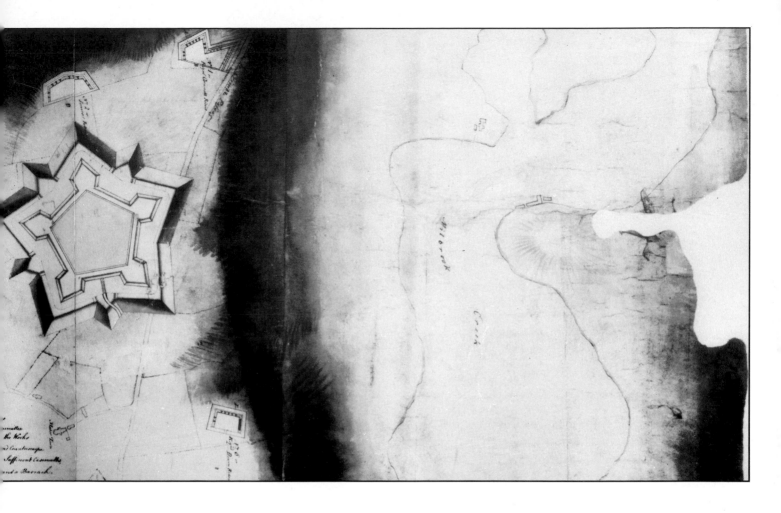

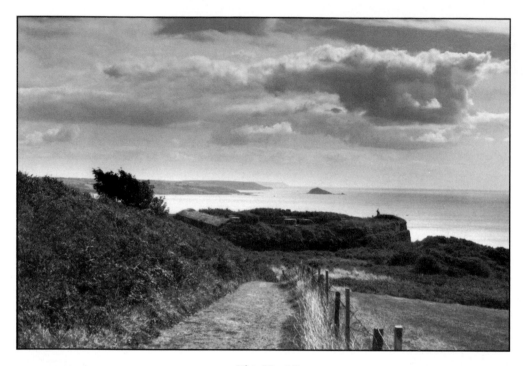

Fig. No.11
The Grenville
(Payne's Fourth or North Gloucester)
Redoubt - see fig.10.

This is the best preserved of the redoubts on Maker Heights and the only one to be built to the specifications indicated on Payne's map. The importance of Maker Heights to the defences of Dock and Plymouth had been realised long before 1783, for Carew, in his survey of Cornwall, informs us that he maintained at his own expense, 170 pike-men, 300 musketeers and 30 cavaliers stationed in this neighbourhood under his command. The forts in this area commanded the whole sweep of Cawsand Bay from Picklecombe Point (the site of a later fort) in the East to Penlee Point in the West. The island rising above the redoubt is the Mewstone, which features in a number of Payne drawings. To the left, somewhat masked by the bush, extends Staddon Heights, where an open battery was established in Payne's time.

Fig. No.12
Record of the marriage of William Payne and Jane Goodridge in Stoke Damerel Church, February 5th, 1785.
Courtesy of the Rector, Stoke Damerel Parish, and the West Devon Record Office, Coxside, Plymouth.

[The Year 1785] Page 403

No 1606 William Payne Draughtsman of the Board of Ordinance & Jane Goodridge of this Parish Spinster were Married in this Church by Licence this Fifth Day of February in the Year One Thousand Seven Hundred and Eighty Five By me [illegible]

This Marriage was ſolemnized between Us { W. Payne / Jane Goodridge

In the Preſence of { [illegible] / Mary Sturt

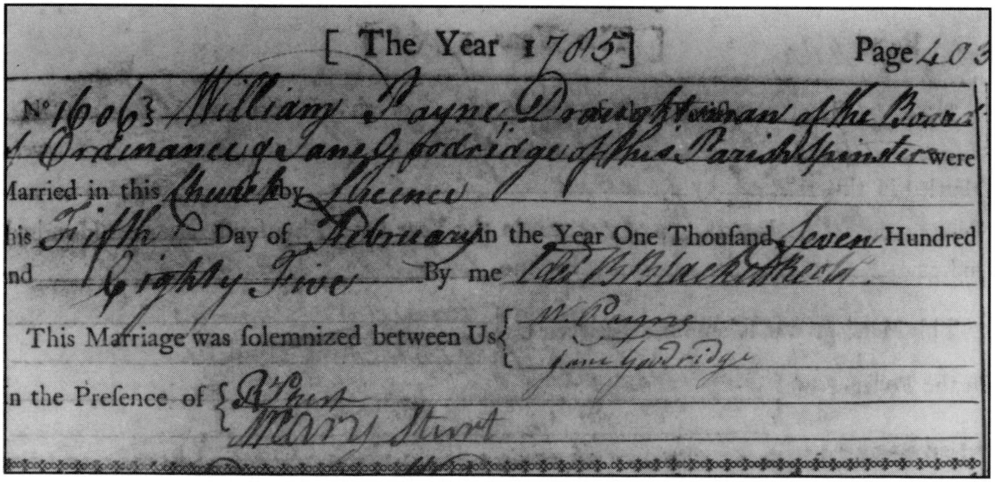

Fig. No.13
Payne's signature on the reverse of the View of Crabtree (no.50).

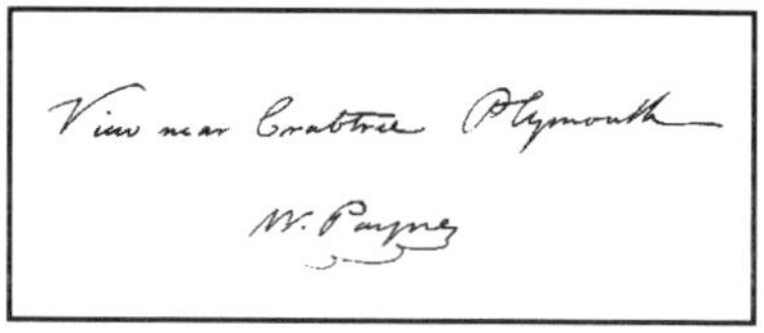

views in, or near, Plymouth. In 1788, there is a view of a slate quarry on Dartmoor, and in 1789, he exhibited two views of Dartmouth and Kingswear. We must remember that the exhibitions represent, in all probability, the preceding year's work. Consequently, the drawings exhibited in 1790, both at the Royal Academy and at the Society of Artists, belong to his Plymouth period, with its distinctive style, as I shall show below in my analysis of these drawings.

On 5th February 1785, William Payne married Jane Goodridge at Stoke Damerel Church. The marriage was by licence and William's parents were not present. We have to remember that it took over two days to reach Plymouth from London in the 1780's and we should not read anything sinister into the absence of his parents. His father could probably not afford to leave his coal business unattended. The witnesses to the marriage were William Payne's fellow Board of Ordnance draughtsman, Robert Sturt and his wife Mary. In the marriage register William Payne gives his occupation as Draughtsman to the Board of Ordnance (spelt Ordinance by the Rector, though in fact this was a recognised spelling in the 18th century) and his signature, written with something of a flourish, is the same one that appears on the reverse of his larger and more important watercolours (figs. 12 & 13). The register states that Jane Goodridge was a "spinster of this parish" but although the name Goodridge does appear in the Plymouth records, her baptismal certificate has not been traced there, though a Jane Goodridge was baptised at Paignton on the 17th February 1763. On 10th January 1786, a son, William Robert, was christened at Stoke Damerel and a second son, Charles, on the 11th February 1787.[45] A third son, Henry, was probably born in Plymouth on 2nd September 1788, but not christened until 24th May 1790 in London.[46]

It was at Plymouth that William Payne's artistic skill developed and the watercolours of this period must now be examined. His work at this time was not primarily concerned with imaginative landscape in the Claudian tradition, though there are echoes of it. All his exhibited works between 1786 and 1790 are of named places except for one—and that is titled *Devotion*. However, we must not read too much into this, for throughout the rest of his life his exhibited pictures are of recognised views, at a time when the bulk of Payne drawings are mere reminiscences of types of landscape. The Plymouth drawings fall into two main categories. The first group are precisely topographical, though often enlivened by the figure interest. In the second, topographical interest is not the sole consideration and figures and landscape complement each other, enhancing the picturesque qualities of the scene. In both, Payne selects his viewpoint with care and arranges his figures to advantage. As such, these composed watercolours are the antithesis of Ordnance Drawings which were intended to be merely accurate—to represent buildings or "cut ground" without the distraction of extraneous elements such as figures. Payne had absorbed too much of the Sandby influence to adopt so stultifying a process. Yet he did not set out to achieve "atmosphere" nor was he seeking to capture the fleeting moment. His immediate purchasers would demand a degree of accuracy: human activity in a place dominated by the life of estuary, port and dockyard were also part of that accuracy. The possibility of reaching a wider audience through engraving had to be borne in mind. By 1788 he had achieved his ambitions in the prints engraved and published by Middiman.

At Plymouth, William Payne found all the elements that appealed to his imagination and temperament. He was attracted to the sea but not to the seascape as such: he remains firmly landlocked. In the same way, he is more at home with the ferryman's craft than the man-of-war. He views the latter on the horizon from the safe viewpoint of the shore, or, if close at hand, at rest in an enclosed and protective anchorage. He is attracted by the irregular roof-line and crumbling masonry of the harbour-cottage; by the estuary with its overhanging rocks, and trees cascading to the water's edge; he introduces the works of man as an effective contrast to the works of nature. On land, he is at home with the toil of the quarryman, and the journeying of the pack-horse carrier; his open landscapes devoid of figure interest tend to emptiness. For that reason, he seldom essays the Dartmoor scene, except from a distance, or unless human activity is attempting in some way to encroach on the loneliness of the view. Indeed, Payne's fascination with the lives of villagers and rustics, in the setting of their crumbling abodes, later so dominant a feature of his output, begins in his Plymouth period.

William Payne initially follows the method of the early topographers. A pen outline is used to mark out the distant hills, the trees in the middle distance and the shape of the buildings. Washes of Indian ink are then applied to denote the simple effects of light and shade before the addition of local colour. As is the case with early topographers, the range of his colours owes much to cartography. Since the earliest dated drawings by Payne seem to belong to the year 1786, style is the only thing we have to go by to identify drawings before that date. He presumably started to depict local scenery in 1783 and in such a drawing as *Looe from the West Looe Road* – perhaps drawn while he was at Maker Heights – his touch is by no means sure. The foreground is too cluttered. The figure moving away to the right is stylised, the horse, waiting patiently for his load, something of a caricature. The hills beyond the town are an unrealistic shade of blue and this colour is repeated on the foreground rock. The boat drawn up on the distant slipway looks like a toy vessel (**1**). Yet most of the elements common to his early drawings are present. He has already discovered the effective trick of "dragging" seen in the patch of clear ground, the warm colouring of which contrasts effectively with the cooler tones around. The scumbling effect is achieved by a brush with drying colour dragged laterally across the paper and leaving many highlights. A vigorous, but not obtrusive pen outlining is used on the foliage behind the path. At this early stage he is using "Payne's grey" for the shadows on the bushes and to enclose the leaves of his tree which frames the composition on the right. Indeed this is already unmistakably a Payne tree, using a simple formula of loops to denote the foliage. Later, Payne

was to discover that the split-brush technique could produce more rapid results. His pen outlining in this example, as in all his Plymouth drawings, is never insistent, as it is in the work of Towne, for example, who always encloses even distant hills with a sharp line. Payne comes closer to Towne in his delineation of the outlines of the houses but here he is merely following his Ordnance training.

More effective are two larger views, *Near Plymouth* and *Looking towards Plympton* in the Exeter collection (**2 & 3**). The second of these is perhaps a little empty and there are few contrasting colours to balance the overwhelming expanse of green and blue-green. However, the distance is well handled and the loops of the distant river in the first picture lead the eye to the far-off sea.

By 1786, Payne was experimenting with a circular or oval format, often in quite small drawings. In *St Nicholas' Island from Obelisk Hill* (**4**), he dispenses with pen outlining on the tree which frames the scene to the right while retaining it for the smaller trees which slant upwards from the left just beyond the field in which two horses graze. The sea is indicated by a series of small, wavy lines. The distant hills stretching from Mount Batten to Staddon Heights are handled with great delicacy, as are the fortifications on the Island itself. Even on this scale he finds room for what is almost a convention in these early drawings—the large leaves of butterbur with which he adorns the immediate foreground. This motif is found in Dutch paintings of the 17th century and in the landscapes of Claude Lorrain, underlying the catholicity of Payne's training. In later drawings Payne replaces the butterbur with a mass of intersecting twigs straggling over rocks.

In a circular drawing, *Plympton St Maurice*, the grey underwash can clearly be seen on the hills beyond the castle (**42**). The colouring on the trees in the middle distance is reminiscent of artists such as Rowlandson and, again, the distant hills above Crabtree are delicately handled. Payne appears to have made a number of versions of this subject, for another circular, and identical version is in Exeter , and a third, variant version is recorded. A still later, though not circular version, from the Devon tour of 1793, is illustrated for a comparison with his later style (**41**).

A view of H. M. Dockyard, also of 1786, is in the Plymouth City Museum (**35**). This, taken from the Battery at Mount Edgcumbe, shows the "Royal Sovereign" and "Glory" on the stocks. Despite the highly formalised waves—Payne was never at his best in portraying surging waves and a choppy sea—this is an impressive picture in the best traditions of topographical painting, not merely portraying the Dockyard from the Cornish side of the Hamoaze, but encapsulating a moment in its history. For just as artists like Rooker, in depicting the crumbling facades of ancient buildings, suggest both their past history and their present fascination for the traveller and antiquary, so Payne is reminding us that the Dockyard existed in the previous century, that many vessels were built there in the past, and that shipbuilding will continue in the future. The figure in the foreground reminds us of the working environment of man and the scale of human activity. A second version is in a private collection.

In the years succeeding 1786, Payne's style matures considerably and he shows increasing confidence in the handling of some quite large watercolours. To this period belongs *Plymouth Dock from Empacombe* (**36**). In this, Payne shows that he does not need the topographical device of a large tree or of a mass of rocks to frame his view. The whole expanse of Plymouth Dock from North Corner to Mount Wise is set out in accurate and minute detail. Here the figures play a more perfunctory role in the scene and in some drawings of this period they are on a smaller scale, somewhat squat, and less sharply in focus. However, he always retains his more carefully drawn figures in his more composed landscapes, where figure interest is crucial to the scene, and where he is aiming at picturesque effects. Some of these drawings are of high quality. In the view of *Smugglers' Cave – a quarry near Plymouth*, which was with the Leger Galleries in 1974, Payne handles the mass of rocks on the quarry face with consummate skill but attention is equally focused on the three figures by the overturned wheelbarrow in the foreground (**26**). Another drawing of the same type and size is *The Bathing Pool, Okehampton* where the mass of foliage enclosing the pool and the figure ascending the steps to the right call for considerable virtuosity. The figure introduces almost a note of humour as the bather's socks obstinately refuse to stay in place (**38**). In both these watercolours, the golden tones, so prevalent in Payne's later works, are apparent, and indeed this is a feature of his Plymouth pictures as he nears the end of his time there. In *Seaton Bridge on the way to Looe* (**15**), he has ample opportunity to offset the cooler tones of his distant trees and of the skilfully drawn cottages straggling up the hill with an expanse of golden sand. In this picture, we note what Long calls "striations or quasi-parallel strokes" in the foreground. Some of these continue for three inches or more. In these early drawings, such striations only appear— and then not often–in the foreground of the composition, and they are never used to add texture to trees in the middle distance, which is his later practice. All these larger pictures, even those that measure 15" x 22" or more, are successful because of the meticulous nature of the draughtsmanship. They are impressive, both as compositions and as topographical records of Plymouth and its environs in the 1780's. By contrast, Payne's later, and looser, style cannot quite sustain pictures of this size and it is his smaller pictures which tend to be more effective.

The watercolours of this, William Payne's first period, continue to the exhibitions of 1789 and 1790, for *The Ruins of Wembury House*, which was with the Leger Galleries in 1973, is almost certainly the picture exhibited at the Society of Artists of Great Britain in 1790 (**46**). In 1789, Sir Joshua Reynolds praised Payne's *Quarry on the Banks of the Plym*, exhibited at the Royal Academy (**75**). As can be seen from the illustration, this is a highly accomplished drawing with numerous figures working at the quarry face, all drawn on quite a small scale. Yet attention focuses on them, as much as on the quarry itself, despite the virtuosity of its handling. Drawings of this sort bridge the gap between topography and romantic landscape.

Many of the early drawings are laid down on Payne's own mounts with a series of broad and narrow lines enclosing a grey wash. A laid paper (generally Whatman) is normally used for the drawing and this is pasted down on another paper of similar type, already prepared with the grey wash border. Sometimes more than one sheet is used. The signatures are always very neat, often much smaller than in his later drawings and sometimes have two vertical dots after the W. I have yet to see a later Payne drawing signed in this way, and another indication of an early Payne drawing is the addition of "Plymouth" after the signature, often in drawings of places at some distance from Plymouth itself. Apart from Dock and Plymouth, most of the drawings of the 1783–9 period are within a six to eight mile radius extending from Looe in the west to Wembury in the east. We should notice that, to the north he visits Lydford and Okehampton, and to the east, beyond Wembury, the Dart and Teign estuaries, as well as Torbay. No doubt Ordnance business accounts for many of the coastal visits (there were batteries both at Dartmouth and at Furzham Down). One drawing, which on stylistic grounds must fall within the period 1789–90, is even further to the east, a view of Weymouth and Portland (**24**).

In the illustrations which follow, and include the drawings mentioned above, I have attempted to chart William Payne's progress as an artist in these early years. There is no doubt that his best pictures were produced in this period, and from 1786 he had attracted, by his exhibited drawings at the Royal Academy, enough attention to be included in S. Middiman's "Select Views in Great Britain" from 1788-9. The engravings after Payne's work included *View on the River Tamar, Trematon Castle, View near Plymouth, Western Mills*, and a *Stone Quarry at Port Elliot (sic), Cornwall*. This would have helped Payne to sell his drawings to both patrons in Plymouth and in London. Amongst the Plymouth patrons were the Yonge family for whom Payne had painted a view of Puslinch House (**18**). This commission and the views of the houses such as the one in the Plympton area, now in Exeter (**3**), were probably the earliest he received. The later patrons were altogether more significant, and towards the end of his time in Plymouth he produced a remarkable series of views of Flete House for the Bulteel family which included not only the house itself but the scenery around the Erme near the house (**9-14**). This was followed in 1789 by views of Cotehele for the newly created Earl of Mount Edgcumbe who had succeeded to the Barony in 1761 and had been made Viscount Mount Edgcumbe and Valletort in 1780. It is surprising that Payne received no commissions from another important family, the Parkers of Saltram, but it has to be remembered that the first Lord Boringdon, the second main patron of Sir Joshua Reynolds (the first was Richard Edgcumbe), died in 1788 and his son was only sixteen at the time. In 1789, Payne had to be content with a record of George III and Queen Charlotte's visit to Mount Edgcumbe, duly exhibited in 1790 at the Royal Academy, though the royal party had made Saltram their base. However, the patronage of all these families must have been helpful to Payne when he returned to London. His work had already caught the eye of Sir Joshua Reynolds, with or without the help of the Edgcumbes and the Parkers. In assessing Payne at this period we must remember that, as he was born in 1760, his drawings are fairly early in the annals of the British School. He operates independently of such artists as Edward Dayes, who only began to exhibit in 1786, and Towne, who was abroad while Payne was receiving his training in London. It is possible that Payne had seen the work of such artists as Hearne and Rooker, born some fifteen years or so before him, but there are few similarities with either, except for a slight affinity in figure drawing in Rooker's case, which can be explained by the Sandby influence. The only other contemporary to note is White Abbott, Towne's pupil, whose first important tour was in 1791. The work of all these artists—though their stature is undeniable—remains stylistically stereotyped over a much longer period than Payne's, whose work advances after a mere six years to a totally separate and distinct style. Payne can hardly be blamed for present-day taste which approves of austerity and patterning, ranking Towne, for example, amongst the very greatest of the English watercolourists. In fact, Payne, in his Plymouth years, produced some remarkable drawings, and it is only their comparative rarity that prevents them from attracting the serious attention that they deserve.

Despite his duties as an Ordnance draughtsman, he found time to paint the scenery he found in Plymouth with affection, in a creative burst of activity. His Ordnance training indicated an approach: the means followed were entirely his own. Though he was not self-taught as such, he produced drawings of skill and individuality. He was profoundly influenced by Plymouth. He had found a wife there and he was to return there, at intervals, during the rest of his life.

3. LONDON: DRAWING MASTER AND ARTIST

William Payne's tour of duty at Plymouth Dock ended, as we have seen, in 1788. Although he records addresses in Dock and London for 1789, he had, in fact, by the end of 1789, obtained a permanent address in London at 2, Thornhaugh Street, Bedford Square.[47] This street does not appear in the St Giles rate books in 1788 and so it was clearly still being built. In 1789, all but three of the houses had been taken, but Payne's name appears in pencil as is often the case with new or later arrivals. The "rent" or rateable value was moderate at £26 per annum and Payne paid £1 8s 2d as the poor rate. It is worth noting that the 18th century Thornhaugh Street ran north from Chenies Street and parallel with Tottenham Court Road, two blocks away from Bedford Square. Thornhaugh Street today is to the north of Russell Square and the 18th century street is now called Huntley Street. There is no doubt that William Payne senior had a hand in this move. The Westminster rate books and the London Trade Directories confirm that he and Eleanor gave up their residence in Park Street at the end of 1789 and moved to a smaller house at Bridge Court, Westminster—now long since gone and roughly in the vicinity of the original New Scotland Yard. William's father may have supported his son financially at this stage, though again it is impossible to say whether the lease of Thornhaugh Street was purchased or if the house was rented.

William Payne exhibited four pictures at the Royal Academy in 1789 and a further four in 1790. No less than sixteen were sent to the Society of Artists of Great Britain in 1790 after a gap of thirteen years. After attracting the favourable notice of Sir Joshua Reynolds, William Payne must have been confident that he could make a living from art, although he knew it could be a precarious existence.

By the end of the century there was a depression in the art market which Farington duly notes. In particular, artists working in the precise style of the topographers' tinted drawings were not finding life easy, unless they reached a wider clientele through engravings, or were able to infuse into their views some of the qualities of the picturesque first hinted at by Gilpin. Thus Hearne contributed to the "Antiquities of Great Britain" and Rooker responded to the texture of crumbling stonework, showing a certain humour, too, in his portrayal of peasants and cattle. Dayes became, par excellence, the artist of the London Square and London fashion. Artists such as William Alexander were chosen to accompany diplomatic missions abroad and enhanced their reputations by the engravings which were produced on their return. By contrast, Paul Sandby's career as an artist, despite a deliberately conscious attempt to work in a looser style in watercolour, or alternatively to embrace more fully the medium of body colour, was beginning to falter. The drawing master, however, was becoming fashionable. By 1790, Paul Sandby had been instructing the gentlemen cadets at Woolwich for over twenty years and the gentry and aristocracy had been introduced, both personally and through a wide variety of published material, to the principles and practice of watercolour painting. There was no reason why these skills should remain the prerogative of the military. The scions of the nobility, youthful amateurs, were prepared to pay for instruction in these arcane accomplishments, as indeed were some aspiring, young, professional artists.

William Payne had probably inherited some of his father's acute business sense, as well as his caution. It would not have been advisable to break with the Ordnance Board too soon. Accordingly, his name appears in the quarterly lists for 1790, albeit almost as an afterthought.[48] From then on, he remains in the Board's service until 1794. Some reorganisation of the Board took place in 1794 and his name appears amongst those on the "New Establishment of the Tower".[49] His position in the lists of the Court and City Register for 1792 and 1793 is revealing, for although he still receives 3s 6d a day, his name is recorded beneath those of draughtsmen who, in 1780, had been junior to him. This would seem to confirm that the Board sanctioned his absence during 1790 and considerable ones thereafter. Always an enlightened and tolerant employer in this respect, they had continued to pay Thomas Sandby's salary although he had long ceased to attend the Tower itself. His duties with the Dukes of Cumberland and Gloucester, quite apart from his position as the first Professor of Architecture at the Royal Academy, would have precluded this. Accordingly, William Payne's position towards the end of the lists suggests that he was allowed considerable freedom where attendance was concerned. Otherwise he could not have established himself as the leading drawing master of the day–and all our sources are in agreement about that–nor could he have undertaken the extensive tours which are reasonably well documented during the years 1790-1793.

William Payne clearly realised that the tight, precise style of his Plymouth watercolours was too demanding a method to be imparted to others, particularly amateurs of moderate accomplishment. What he needed was a simplified version of his approach, retaining the tricks which produced effect without labour. He had returned from the West Country with a store of drawings and sketches which could be adapted to the requirements of picturesque embellishment. Already there are signs of reappraisal in the later Plymouth drawings. We can observe greater breadth in the handling of the rock scenery in the *Quarry on the Banks of the Plym* (**75**). The contrast of dark foreground against light distance becomes more pronounced and is often handled with great skill, as is the case with his drawing of Weymouth and Portland (**24**). He was not yet ready, however, to abandon the topography of the actual scenery for made up views which would serve as models for pupils, and the signed drawings we possess for the years 1790-1791 remain broadly topographical, though transitional in technique. We may surmise that he divided the summer months of these years between Devon and London for there are signed and dated drawings of Denham Bridge and Western Mills near Plymouth and of the windmills near Blackheath.[50] As he was in London for the baptism of his third and fourth sons, Henry and George, at St Giles-in-the-Fields, Holborn on 5th May,[51] any tour of Devon would have been of short duration in view of his return to the Drawing Room at the Tower.

It is, however, in the tours of 1791-3 that Payne develops the distinctive style of his second period and the one that he imparts to his pupils. I have already mentioned his business sense. For just as his father moved to an area where the houses of the great, with a full complement of servants, would in the London season consume a vast amount of coal (and indeed they remained staffed throughout the year), so his son saw that by becoming the drawing master of the fashionable, his autumn and winter months would be fully occupied in teaching, leaving the summer clear for his tours and the search for suitable subject matter. The West Country was at hand. So too was Wales, and by 1793 he had added the Principality to his list of places rich in coastal scenery. For it is worth noting that whereas later practitioners, such as Varley, were drawn to the mountain scenery of Wales—and indeed the Cymrian view becomes very much the stock in trade of pioneer artists of the British School—Payne sticks initially very much to the south and west coast of Wales and proceeds no further north than Cardigan (a Conway scene is not recorded until 1812): with more daring, he penetrates further inland but only to the river valleys, discovering in particular an affinity with the Usk, the Wye, and the Teifi. These, together with some visits further afield, to which we will return later, are a feature of his output over the next thirty five years.

The drawings of 1791 and the next two years bear out Pyne's reference to "his subjects in small… brilliant in effect and executed with spirit". He is from now on effective in small watercolours (about 6" x 8") which set out to achieve atmosphere. In the drawings of his Plymouth period he had portrayed the local scene with sharpness of vision and in bright light, with the lowering clouds which are plentiful in this rain soaked area hinted at or relegated to the perimeter of his compositions. He now becomes adept at recording misty effects or shafts of slanting light which help to enhance the contrasts of dark foreground against lighter middle distance with a receding landscape dissolving into vaporous light beyond. He introduces clouds scurrying across the sky with an economy of means, often taking a wash of gamboge across the whole to show sunlight effects in late evening. That golden tones predominate is not, as has been suggested, the result of fading indigos, but because Payne consciously chooses to bathe his pictures in such a light. It is true, of course, that the fading of his greens and blues sometimes suggests a colour scheme out of balance, and that is the price he pays for the introduction of indigo. He uses it sparingly, if at all, in his Plymouth pictures and their condition, at least where fading is concerned, is usually good in comparison with his later works.

Enough Welsh drawings are dated 1791 to make it clear that Payne visited the south coast of Wales at this time, probably in conjunction with West Country tours, for dated drawings in both areas are recorded. The possibility that he was there on Board of Ordnance business cannot be ruled out. Records are silent about this area until 1797, when an Irish-American adventurer, General Tate, landed with French soldiers at Fishguard and was promptly arrested by the local militia. Leaving this aside, we can say that Payne proceeded along the south coast of Wales in 1791, for dated drawings include views of Aberavon and Swansea. In the 1937 exhibition of Payne's work at Plymouth, 53 of the 140 framed watercolours were Welsh views and some of these, though the majority were undated, must have resulted from this tour, which, from their titles, we can tentatively reconstruct. Crossing the Severn at the Aust Ferry, he proceeded via Chepstow to Caerleon and thence to Caerphilly and arrived at Bridgend after a detour to Lantrisant and Pontypridd. He next visited the twin villages of Newton and Nottage (condensed in his inscription to Newton Notage), and from there he went via Neath to Aberavon where the copper works engaged his interest (**79**). In this picture he has not dispensed with pen outlining totally, for he encloses the sails of the small vessel putting out to sea with a firmly drawn line. This small drawing (5" x 6 5/8") is a successful composition and the figures are well grouped and help to animate the scene. Swansea via Britton Ferry may well have been the end of this particular trip, but if the possibility of an Ordnance tour is borne in mind, this could explain the views of Tenby, Pembroke, Fishguard and Cardigan which appear from time to time in his Welsh drawings, for there are batteries on the coast between Pembroke and Fishguard which he may have visited. It is possible that on this tour, visits further afield were undertaken, for he seems to have made his way up the Wye as far as Ross after visiting Monmouth, and from Caerleon he traced the Usk up as far as Brecon. Likewise the visit to Swansea may have prompted a visit to Dynevor.

Payne seems to have returned to Wales in succeeding years, for views on the Usk and Wye, and at Brecon, are recorded in 1792 and 1793. If the Brecon picture resulted from an actual visit and is not a studio drawing worked up from a previous sketch, Payne may well have visited Wales from North Devon, for a Devon tour of 1793 is well documented.

1793 appears to have been an annus mirabilis for Payne, for there are many dated drawings this year, including some large and impressive worked up watercolours (**49 & 50**). Above all, there are two volumes of views, once owned by the Rev. John Swete of Oxton House near Dawlish, a keen amateur artist and possibly a Payne pupil. Swete, whose name originally was Tripe, changed his name on receiving an inheritance. If he did have lessons from Payne, it is likely that he received them at Oxton House, for there is a drawing of the house in the first volume and a quite separate view, dated 1793, of the quarry nearby (**51**) which suggests that Payne made Oxton the base for drawings in the immediate vicinity. These volumes are now in the Westcountry Studies Library at Exeter and as the drawings have not been exposed to light, their colours are still fresh. The size of each of these drawings is 5" x 6½", but they are by no means outdoor sketches. Payne's normal practice, to judge from a series of Devon views, dated 1825, was to make a monochrome wash drawing as a basis for worked up drawings (**84 & 85**). The drawings in these volumes, presenting as they do the full gamut of Payne's mannerisms, require, with their small scale, precision in draughtsmanship and carefully controlled colouring. To underline the point, there is no clear chronological arrangement, as an examination of the titles given in Appendix V makes clear. For, although the first four drawings include Oxton House and the other three are of places nearby, the next seven, of Torquay and adjacent areas, are juxtaposed with views of the Taw in North Devon. For this reason, it is impossible to say where Payne started this tour and we can only note the main areas in which he operated and the likely base for each. My own feeling is that Payne began in Exeter, visiting the coast to the south via Topsham and going east as far as Beer. Returning to Exeter, he moved to Oxton, which became a base for visits to the coast at Torquay and Brixham and later up the Dart. In 1789, Swete had travelled to North Devon from Oxton and his itinerary looks remarkably similar to Payne's.[52] Payne could possibly have followed this route on Swete's advice, returning to Plymouth via Torrington, Okehampton and Tavistock. Alternatively, the Plymouth visit could have preceded the journey to North Devon, allowing Payne to proceed to South Wales on one of the boats plying between Ilfracombe and Neath. In the 18th century, artists like Payne, travelling on horseback or by coach and diligence, expected to stay in country houses and there are fourteen such views, in the two volumes, seven of them recording their owner's names.

The very existence of these tours in these crowded years of 1791-93 must have cast doubt on the established tradition that Payne, encouraged by the fact that his fame had preceded him, was able to establish himself as the most fashionable drawing master in London almost overnight. My own view is that this was a gradual process which accelerated rapidly on his return from the 1793 tour. He had ceased to exhibit in 1790 and was not to do so again for nineteen years–an incredibly long period for any artist wishing to keep his name before the public. The tours were essential. He had to work out a new approach; above all he had to work rapidly. It was this new style which enabled him to become a drawing master for, as Pyne says, he had reduced the principles of landscape to a system which could be imparted to others. The tours are an integral part of that system. They are made effective by it, and they, in their turn, make it effective as a medium for teaching.

That Payne was already known as a teacher is shown by the fact that John Glover, at that stage an aspiring young artist, sought lessons from him in London. This emerges in Farington's Diary for December 30th 1794, for Farington tells us that Glover had made four visits to London prior to that date, though he does not tell us in which year he received these lessons, which amounted in all to eight. As a result, we are told, Glover was able to establish himself as a teacher. From Farington's account, we also learn that it was the practice of the fashionable teacher to visit the houses of his well-to-do clients. Moreover, as Glover was able to charge two guineas a day for a visit to one house or one guinea each when he went to two houses, we have a useful starting point for determining Payne's charges, which must have been in excess of this initially, and considerably more by 1794. In any case, Payne would have visited more than one household each day. Although we cannot be certain how much he earned during these years, his annual earnings are likely to have been high. A provincial drawing master like Francis Towne, Farington notes in his Diary for 1st November 1796, could earn as much as £500 per year at Exeter. Later, in the 19th century, John Varley was reputed to have made £3,000 from teaching and sales of pictures.[53] By 1794, therefore, William Payne's earnings must have exceeded £500. His house in Thornhaugh Street was well placed for visits to the fashionable squares of London, though Pyne's list should not be regarded as definitive but merely as an indication of the social circles in which Payne was able to operate.

As for his teaching methods, Payne may have used the system later adopted by his own pupil, Glover. For Farington, in his Diary for April 20th 1808, tells us that Glover "begins a drawing, his pupil standing by, and having proceeded as far as he considers it to be a lesson, leaves it with his pupil to copy."

However, an alternative clue to Payne's teaching practice emerges from a series of grey wash drawings, extensively inscribed with colour notes, which appeared on the market recently. The drawings were simple compositions, some showing a castle on a bluff, above a wooded landscape. The colour notes were detailed enough to enable pupils to produce a finished drawing from the monochrome base.

By the end of the century, and in the first decade of the 19th century, when drawing masters had proliferated, it was more customary for the wealthy amateur to visit the residence of the artist. This emerges from some biographical notes on Francis Nicholson by a member of his family, which provides an undoubted insight into the later teaching practice of William Payne.[54] We can only regret the absence of such anecdotal information about Payne himself:

It became an absolute craze among ladies of fashion to profess landscape painting. They eagerly paid their guinea an hour for the privilege of witnessing the progress of a picture by their favourite professor. To such a degree was this mania carried that every hour of the day was devoted to this easy and lucrative employment, and the more difficulty there was found in obtaining permission, the greater of course became the anxiety to gain it. No time was too early, no hour too late, for receiving what was called a lesson.

One lady found that 8 a.m. was the only time available for a lesson, from which she returned an hour later to continue her slumbers.

It is idle to speculate about the names of Payne's aristocratic pupils, though tradition records some of them. Pyne tells us that he became all the rage and implies that these youthful and noble amateurs were numerous.[55] Amongst them were the Grenville family, for in the 1936 sale at Warwick Castle there were a number of drawings by members of that family in Payne's style. His pupils naturally included aristocratic young ladies and a relative of the Duke of Northumberland is mentioned in this context in the 1937 Plymouth catalogue. More recently, drawings in Payne's style from the collection of Lady Louisa Kerr, whose mother, the Countess of Antrim, was said to be Payne's pupil, were sold at Christie's. The album contained a small landscape by Payne himself inscribed in Lady Antrim's hand "Payne sketch" (**61**). Other authorities quote Payne-type drawings by a J.M. Perry, J. Burbank and Captain Humphreys, and Major General John Gaspard Le Marchant is said to have been his pupil. Apart from this no definitive list of his amateur pupils, aristocratic or otherwise, can reasonably be given. A clearer connection can be found with some professional artists. The best known pupil is Glover, who clearly absorbed some of Payne's mannerisms. The split brush technique for the rapid delineation of foliage and the oblique shaft of light illuminating the middle distance are obvious examples. A comparison of two drawings, Payne's *Weir on the Tamar* from the 1793 tour and Glover's *On the River Lledr* show both the similarities and the differences (**66 & 100**). Glover departs from Payne in his treatment of the trees clinging to the rocks beyond the river and in the use of short brush strokes on the hills, though some of the washes on the boulders strewn on the bank and in the stream itself are close to Payne's method. Glover's work in this vein is often overloaded, but this example is redeemed by his romantic response to the scene before him and by the rich autumnal colouring he uses. Payne's methods are more economical but, despite his penchant for gamboge, the overall effect is often colder. Payne could not have produced a drawing like this, for such scenery did not appeal to him. It was, however, suited to Glover's temperament, for he had, no doubt, been introduced to the mountain scenery of Wales by his other mentor, "Warwick" Smith,[56] and was able to apply the skills he had learned from both teachers to the new notions of the sublime. Other artists working more or less in Payne's style include J. H.

Harding, an example of whose work is illustrated,(**99**) and in some of his rare landscapes, William Anderson. At Plymouth, an obscure watercolourist, T. H. Williams, works in a version of Payne's style.[57] (**97**) All these were operating by the end of the 18th century, but that Payne's influence extended well into the 19th century is shown by the career of Sebastian Pether (born 1780) whose work recalls Payne's not infrequent moonlight scenes (**48**).

Another artist whose early work is frequently compared with Payne's and who has been mentioned before, is Francis Nicholson. Nicholson, of course, was older than Payne by some six years or so, and had attracted notice in the 1780's by his views of Whitby, Scarborough and other places in Yorkshire. He had set himself up as a drawing master in London at a later date than Payne, probably not before 1802. It is possible that his work before then was influenced by Payne, though it seems doubtful to me that he took lessons from him. Martin Hardie and other writers draw attention to the cold tonality of Nicholson's work at this period due to his use of grey and blue-grey and his penchant for Payne-like foregrounds. He preferred, however, to use rather sickly greens and yellows in his foliage which is at variance with Payne's practice and his work tended to woolliness at times. For the sake of comparison I have illustrated a well known work by Nicholson, *The Dropping Well at Knaresborough,* which reveals both the similarities and the differences (**101**). Despite this, confusions can still occur. In the Victoria and Albert Museum there are four drawings, traditionally ascribed to Payne, which are difficult to fit into his œuvre. Two are views of Scarborough, one from the North, the other from the South, and two are river scenes of St Paul's, from Westminster Bridge and below London Bridge respectively. All are notable for their carefully drawn architectural details with clear, firm washes enclosed within pen outlines. Long commented that the reddish tones in the middle distance of the watercolours reminded him of certain works by Nicholson, though he did not question the attribution to Payne. However, the treatment of the foreground foliage, with a rather fussy pen line, in the Scarborough drawings is remarkably similar to that in the Knaresborough view. The existence of another Scarborough view from the South, which was with Christie's in 1978 and firmly attributed to Nicholson, should also be taken into account, for not only were the figures and their disposition virtually identical, but the Christie's drawing showed traces of an etched outline, a common practice with Nicholson for the duplication of scenes of Scarborough and elsewhere (**102 & 103**).

The London scenes present a more intractable problem (**104 & 105**). As far as the Westminster view is concerned, the dark foreground and its liberal use of grey are reminiscent of Payne, but the drawing of the figures (and here again comparisons with *The Dropping Well* are instructive) is closer to Nicholson, with an obtrusive pen line round them which is at variance with Payne's practice. The subject matter of the two London drawings imposes tighter constraints than the Scarborough drawings, suggesting a much more competent hand. However, noting Nicholson's penchant for duplication by the etched outline process, I began to look for further examples of these scenes, and although another version of the Westminster drawing has yet to appear, a second example of the London Bridge view, with etched outline, was with Christie's in 1977, again correctly attributed to Nicholson. This drawing was less firmly handled and the reworking of the figures too crude to be by Payne, for although Payne also adopted the etched outline process in the year 1790, the hand is always clearly his and confusions are impossible. Furthermore, the two London drawings and one of the Scarborough views are laid down on lined paper with elaborate wash mounts in which the wider band of grey is complemented by two narrower bands of green and red. This combination is found on the mounts of other undisputed Nicholson drawings, whereas Payne tends to prefer more sober colours. On balance, I think all four drawings should be reattributed, for if either artist were copying the other's scenes, such reworkings would suggest plagiarism rather than deference.

Payne's most obvious pupil is his son, William Robert, who exhibited first in 1802.[58] An unsuccessful and, as will be shown later, impecunious artist, he only appears to have exhibited once again, at Suffolk Street in 1845. I have seen one drawing by William Robert: a crudely drawn estuary scene, dated 1797, it was entirely consistent with the work of a moderately gifted twelve year old working in his father's style.

Some elements of that style have already been mentioned. As it was to persist at least until 1825, a closer analysis must now be given. The account in Redgrave's "Century of Painters" provides a good starting point:

Payne adopted many peculiarities in his methods of execution, some of which are valuable additions to the art. He abandoned the use of outline with the pen. His general process was very simple. Having invented a grey tint (still known by the colour-men as Payne's grey), he used it for all the varied gradations of his middle distance, treating the extreme distance, as also the clouds and the sky, with blue. For the shadow, in his foreground, he used Indian ink or lampblack, breaking these colours into the distance by the admixture of grey. In this he differed but slightly from the other artists of his time, but his methods of handling were peculiarly his own. These consisted in splitting the brush to give the forms of foliage, dragging the tints to give texture to his foreground, and taking out the forms of lights by wetting the surface and rubbing with bread or rag. He seems to have been among the first who used this practice, which, in the hands of Turner, became such a powerful aid to effect, and enabled the early painters in watercolour to refrain from using white or solid pigments in the lights.

Having thus prepared a vigorous light and shade, Payne tinted his distance, middle distance and foreground with colour, retouching and deepening the shadows in front to give power to his work, and even loading his colour and using gum plentifully.

There is little in this account to criticise, though Redgrave does not analyse Payne's method of "dragging", a device already present in his Plymouth period. Pyne, however, in a passage considerably more generous than any already quoted, had earlier provided a detailed description in the " Magazine of the Fine Arts," 1832:

> *It should be observed that the ingenious inventor of this style contrived to use the painting-brush for the foreground in a way that he termed "dragging", namely, on its side, which dexterously applied, left a number of accidental lights, very useful and characteristic of pebbles on the sea shore, or for a gravelled road, and particularly effective in producing the roughness on the surface of rocks, or the texture of the bark of trees. The whole being carefully tinted, by a judicious washing and blending, which must be done by passing lightly over the whole with a painting brush moderately saturated with pure water, the drawing is then ready for the finishing touches. This last operation is performed by taking advantage of those accidents and lights which the drag of the brush has left, and by undertouching and adding spirit to the shadows with Cologne-earth or Vandyck-brown, separately, or mixed with the other tints as may be necessary; and by this simple process in proportion to the taste and judgment of the operator, will the drawing be valuable as a work of art. This may be justly said of the process; —that, applied by the amateur who is an adept at execution, and imbued with a taste for design, very delightful drawings may be wrought thereby. The style of Payne, indeed, is so eminently calculated for producing effect with facility that it is peculiarly suited to the amateur who practises landscape drawing merely for amusement.*

William Payne's technique was a variation of the earlier topographers' practice. Where they, and he, in his earlier drawings, used Indian ink in various dilutions to paint in shadows, from 1790 onwards, Payne uses "Payne's grey" both for this purpose and to block in the middle distance. He had already discovered this device in his Plymouth period, though he uses it sparingly then, mostly for the underlying loops of foliage on the trees which frame his compositions, a practice he continues to use. This, together with the richer and, particularly, golden colours which surround this grey wash or are superimposed, adds opulence to his watercolours. He replaces the colder colour scheme of his earlier drawings with warmer tints, which are particularly suited to morning or late evening effects where lengthening shadows in the foreground enable him to point his contrasts. None of these devices would have been possible without the advances made in paper manufacture towards the end of the 18th century and in the preparation of pigments. The much stronger wove papers enabled Payne to take out lights by wetting and rubbing the surface– an impossible process on the earlier laid papers. In addition, the smoother surface of some papers encouraged him to work on a small scale while the newer pigments introduced by the colourmen enabled him to achieve richer tones. W.H. Pyne attributed most of these advances to Turner and Girtin, ignoring Payne, who certainly used them at an earlier date. Admittedly, Payne did not break totally with the early topographers' practice and "use local colour… shadowing the same with the individual tint of its own shadow" as Turner and Girtin did, following in this respect artists like Cozens, and, to a certain extent, Towne, who had already initiated the practice. More often Payne, though adding some of his own shadows after the application of local colour, is content to use grey for the purpose. In many of his drawings, Payne works with a well-charged brush, reserving delicacy for his distances. In nearly all, whether small or large, the lighter areas beyond the immediate foreground are broken by "dragging" and "striations". The latter are sometimes drawn with a ruler, and in drawings of this period they are added to trees and rocks in the middle distance, where, instead of parallel strokes, they frequently intersect each other. More frequently, however, and here I take issue with Long, they are not produced by the same process—or a variant of it—as the foreground striations, but by saturating a piece of textured cloth or sacking with colour and placing it over the already dry colour. It is this process which produces the regular criss-cross patternings often seen in his middle distances, and Payne does not always use it sparingly: the pictures of his 1793 Devon tour are full of this device which, seen en masse, tends to be wearisome. Payne was sometimes not too careful in cutting this textured material to the right size before applying broken colour to the required areas and the patterning frequently extends into the spaces surrounding the silhouette of the trees or rocks (**45**). It was this sort of invention, together with the split brush technique, that enabled Payne to impart the tricks of his trade to pupils. He had invented short-hand devices which enabled striking effects to be gained quickly: in the wrong hands they can become mannered, as is the case with drawings in the style of Payne which are the work of unnamed pupils. Together with this landscape technique, Payne also simplified his figure drawing. These figures, with their characteristic small dots for eyes, are not unlike those of Ibbetson, though they tend to lack the character and sense of movement that Ibbetson brings to them (**98**). Nonetheless, they are effectively grouped and accompanied, as they frequently are, by packhorses, donkeys and dogs, they add interest and colour to his scenes, the men often wearing red or blue coats, and the women, red blouses. Indeed there was a tradition in the 19th century, recorded by a Plymouth artist Henry Incledon Johns, whose father worked in the Dockyard during Payne's time there, that the artist persuaded one old man, who habitually wore a red coat, to pose for him.[59] The same colour scheme is used by Payne in the soft ground etchings he issued from Thornhaugh Street in 1792 (**94**). Earlier in 1790 he issued a set of prints of slightly smaller format (7" x 10½" as against 11" x 15" approximately), in which the colouring is closer to the drawings of his Plymouth period (**92 & 93**). All of these he presented as watercolours, laying them on his characteristic grey wash mounts, a process which he adopts later for small, hand-coloured aquatints, produced by engravers like J. Hassell, S. Alken, and for publishers such as John P. Thompson of Great Newport Street (**95 & 96**). It is the production of these which enabled Payne, despite the lack of exhibited works until 1809, to enhance his reputation. It is interesting that the earliest prints were issued from Thornhaugh Street, for this suggests that Payne may have exhibited drawings, worked up from his tour material, at this address. Others, no doubt, were made available for copying, a common practice with drawing masters. Long suggests that the firm of Random and Stainbrook of 17 Old Bond Street, lent original drawings as well as the aquatints by Hassell for aspiring artists to copy.[60]

From 1794 onwards it is extremely difficult to give any account of Payne's tours to the West Country, Wales or further afield and the details of his life can only be given in outline. It is unlikely that he undertook any tour in 1794 as his father fell ill in the early summer and died in August. In his Will, the full details of which I give in Appendix I, he left Eleanor his coals and barges which were presumably disposed of as the name of Payne disappears at this point from the trade directories. Some time previously Payne's father had purchased two properties at Greenwich, one freehold and one leasehold. The leasehold house, No. 22 Royal Hill, was left in trust to Eleanor for his second grandson, Charles, and the freehold property to his son. As William Robert received a gold watch in his grandfather's Will, the freehold house, or the proceeds from its sale, would, presumably, have been passed on to him in due course, after being held in trust by his father. All the grandchildren, those already born and yet to be born, were to benefit from the sale of four percent stock at the Bank of England. Small bequests were left to Jane, his son's wife, and to his own sisters resident in Burwash, Hawkhurst and Rye. At the time of his father's Will, William and Jane had added a daughter to their four sons—Harriet, baptised at St Giles-in-the-Fields on 3rd January 1794—and then they had three more children, Edward, baptised on 10th November 1794, Jane Charlotte, baptised on 12th August 1796 and finally Frederick, baptised on 9th January 1800.[61] With five children by 1794, a total of eight later, the proceeds of William Payne senior's four percent would hardly have gone far – all the more so as his Will indicates only a moderate degree of prosperity. William Payne's own Will suggests that he re-invested this sum of money in the Bank of England's new four percent stock at a later date, duly passing on the proceeds to his children who had not at the time been provided for.

Payne's upbringing as the son of a coal merchant with barges plying constantly on the Thames from the Pool of London up to Westminster Bridge, helps to explain why coastal and estuary views, throughout the whole of his artistic career, form a significant part of his output. His tour of duty in Plymouth confirmed that interest.

There are, however, other more complex influences on Payne's artistic development. Payne's acquaintance with the conventions of 17th Century Dutch seascapes emerges in the figure drawing of his early period. The Dutch vision was essentially a comforting one: the bustling activity, on vessels afloat, or on the seashore, made the elemental forces of nature seem less forbidding. With that vision Payne's temperament was wholly in accord. His concentration at this time on linear and stylised formulae for the delineation of waves and precipitous cliffs assists in taming the riot of nature. As he leaves his Plymouth period behind, there is a perceptible shift in attitude. This owes much to the development in the 1790's by Sir Uvedale Price and other writers of Gilpin's theory of the picturesque and its relationship to the sublime and the beautiful.[62] With the early theory and its suggested rearrangement of the elements of nature to produce a wholly imaginary and generalised sublimity, Payne would have had little sympathy. Price, however, was advocating irregularity of contour, moss-strewn rocks, broken palings, and crumbling masonry in his new notions of the picturesque, together with autumnal tonality. With that view, as he developed his new style, Payne had more

in common. Furthermore, in his "Essay on the Picturesque", produced between 1794 and 1798, Price had advanced the view that women near a waterfall, washing clothes on a river bank, afforded an image of peace and security. Steeped, as he was, in classical literature, Price was prepared, in support of his theory, to quote Homer, who presents such mundane activities as an oasis of calm in a world of frenzied heroic conflict. Such a view was attractive too, in a period menaced by warfare and revolution, and probably struck a chord with Payne, who had as much reason as anyone to appreciate the ever-present threat to this country's coastal security. Although some of the elements outlined by Price in the 1790's had been anticipated in Payne's earlier work, it is worth noting that rustics engaged in their everyday tasks, including washerwomen, become a recurring motif in the later drawings (**58**). He accords them a greater diversity of activity, and shows an increasing interest in landscape, although the sea is never far away. But this more homely view precludes the sublime. Though he played his part in the broadening concept of marine art, he avoided the ultimate manifestation of the sublime in marine terms, eschewing, for the most part, raging seas and shipwrecks. Where landscape is concerned, in his Welsh tours he seems initially to avoid those areas deemed sublime by the cognoscenti. Although castles engage his attention, antiquarian interests are probably paramount, for he has some knowledge of Camden, quoting him on at least one Welsh drawing. He kept away from the Lakes–a favoured area for travellers in search of the sublime–until he was in his fifties. In place of the sublime we have hermits, beggars, and country folk set in a landscape of some disorder. Here, perhaps, he begins to part from Price's theories, as there is more than a hint that this disorder pervades the lives of these rustics. For in another context, on the seashore or secluded estuary creek, they are often engaged in the time-honoured business of smuggling–an interest which may go back to childhood days; Burwash, his father's birthplace, was a notorious haunt of smugglers. This interest in the villagers and their occupations also separates Payne from those purveyors of the cottage scene working in the tradition of artists like Ruisdael. He may portray gnarled oaks and suggest a riot of nature threatening to overwhelm these vulnerable abodes, but it is the rustics themselves who engage his attention.

Payne must have realised that his skill lay in portraying such scenes as these and he seems to have confined his tours to Wales and the West Country until 1802, when his son, who was only seventeen at the time, exhibited a coastal view of the Isle of Wight. His tours outside these areas do not result in convincing drawings, as is shown by the scenes he painted in the Lake District, which he first visited in 1811, returning there in 1819 or 1820. By 1809, he was very much the established drawing master and, accordingly, when he begins exhibiting again, his prices are high by the standards of the day, though by that time his pupil Glover's prices were just as high. By then he had joined the Old Water Colour Society as an Associate on 13th February 1809, though he only remained in it for four years, resigning in 1813. 1812 was a crisis year for the Society and its decision to admit oils from 1813 was probably too much for Payne, as it was for some other artists. He probably considered the Royal Academy and the British Institution to be the proper recipients of oil paintings as well as watercolours and felt that the O.W.C.S. should confine itself to the medium for which it had been established. Alternatively, he may have felt slighted at not becoming a full member. In the four years, his prices ranged from £3 3s 0d, presumably for small watercolours, to £42 for large, highly finished works, and in 1809, the two most expensive works were sold on the twenty third and forty third day respectively to G.W. Leeds Esq.[63] It is strange that Payne did not sell to aristocratic patrons–though the suffix Esquire implies someone from the landed gentry–and the names of other purchasers of Payne drawings at the Society suggest middle class patrons, indicating a shift in patronage that was beginning at this period and was to become more marked later.

In 1808, increasing prosperity and the demands of a growing family necessitated a move to a larger house near Thornhaugh Street, at No. 10 North Crescent, where the "rent" was £90 a year, giving a rate of £10 6s 3d per annum.[64] However, this was clearly an interim move for within two years Payne had purchased the lease of a house in the rapidly expanding and highly fashionable area of Marylebone at No. 49, Upper Baker Street.[65] These houses, near Regent's Park, were sought after, expensive and part of an area which a contemporary historian stated to be "distinguished beyond all London for regularity, the breadth of the streets, and the respectability of the inhabitants, the majority of whom are titled persons, and those of the most ancient families".[66] Baker Street itself seems to have attracted not merely such people, but artists and members of the acting profession.

In earlier times the area of Marylebone had been the home of Romney, Richard Wilson, and of the Westcountrymen, Opie and Ozias Humphrey. Later, as the area attracted a high proportion of London's artists, it became the home of John Martin, Payne's nearest neighbour, and more notably of Constable and Turner. Richard Cosway, another Westcountry artist, was still in residence when Payne moved there, living in some ostentation at Stratford Place–an altogether more patrician address. Most of the houses in the area had been built over the last thirty years or so, but numbers 46-49 in Upper Baker Street were still being built in 1810, as the rate books state, and Payne's name is not recorded until 1811. The rent or rateable value was £70 and the house was assessed for four rates rather than the usual two, for, in addition to the Poor Rate of £6 2s 6d, and a paving rate, Payne paid a "watch" rate and one for "repairing, cleansing and lighting". This is revealing, for Marylebone prided itself on its cleanliness and amenities. By 1810 a feature of Marylebone was the patrolling of night watchmen with their lanterns as they set out from the Marylebone Watch House. Their job was to clear the streets of undesirables and drunkards as well as to call the time in the small hours.

By 1810, when he moved to Upper Baker Street, William Payne had reached the peak of his career, but it is doubtful if he managed to sustain the level of his earnings over the next ten years, let alone over the remaining twenty of his life. He had certainly taken up oil painting to a greater extent than before, as can be seen from his exhibits at the British Institution which began in 1809 and continued to 1830 with a three year gap from 1817-1819 and one in 1828. Four views exhibited between 1809 - 1812 were more than 4ft by 6ft. Out of a total of fifty exhibits, probably at least sixteen were oils. One, a view on the Wye, exhibited in 1810 (cat. no. 220), is probably the picture of that name now in Exeter (**90**). This seems to bear out Colonel Grant's assertion that Payne's oils are painted in a similar style to the watercolours. Most seem to be not far removed in tonality from some of the larger, worked-up watercolours of his second period. Some, however, are more dashing in execution and of an altogether lighter palette, possibly following the stylistic change which occurs in Payne's watercolours in the 1820's. The catalyst for this may be a series of Italian drawings begun in 1818 which, in turn, may be Payne's response to the work of other artists who were leaving him behind in both colour and technique.

An examination of all the pictures exhibited by Payne from 1809 to 1830 reveals that thirty seven were views of Wales or on the Wye, while twenty five were of Devon or Cornwall. The remaining nine included four views of the Lakes, two of the Thames, one Italian view, one landscape composition and one entitled *Banditti*. The size of the watercolours at the British Institution was also large, indicating in these years a number of studio works. As none of these pictures are dated, it is difficult to recreate William Payne's tours at this time, apart from the visit to the Lakes, already referred to. In addition, the increasing number of his watercolours in the 19th century, which appear to be mere reminiscences of scenery based on West Country and Welsh drawings, would seem to indicate that he had cut down on the number and extent of his tours.

The Italian pictures remained a puzzle for earlier writers, until 1977 when six from the series were sold at Christie's. It emerged that Payne, together with Varley and Copley Fielding, was commissioned by an amateur artist, John Trower, to make copies of drawings he had made on a tour of Italy and Switzerland. The majority of these were dated 1818 and, in deference to their subject matter, were in a higher range of colours, with purple predominating, than is usual in Payne drawings (**87, 88 & 89**). These watercolours show that in the last decades of his life William Payne was still, in some quarters, appreciated enough to attract an important commission. The total number of these pictures is probably about thirty. Some eight years later when he was sixty six, we find Payne revisiting North Devon and Wales. It is to this year that a series of monochrome wash drawings belongs. Elsewhere I have mentioned that it was Payne's habit to work in this way before proceeding to finished coloured drawings–a common habit in any case with water colourists. A number of these were in Payne's possession at the time of his death as is confirmed in his Will. At about the same time, Payne begins to paint small pictures in body colour, on either brown or white paper, and in a higher range of colour. These pictures, mostly views in Devon and Wales, constitute a further change in style, with the figures as well grouped as ever, and sunset effects in some quite rich colouring (**82 & 83**). Although these pictures are an attempt to break new ground they remain very much the work of an 18th century artist attempting to escape from a stylistic straitjacket. Their heightened colour apart, these pictures, on the evidence of their figure drawing, could have been painted at any time during Payne's career. It is fortunate that enough are dated to 1825 or 6 to mark them out as the third and final phase of his artistic achievement. To the same period must belong the self portrait in oils which is in The Castle Museum, Nottingham (see frontispiece). It shows the artist, apparently in his sixties, gazing at us somewhat severely from behind his spectacles, though there is a hint of a more benign nature lurking in the severity. This is a good, though not outstanding portrait, and, in painting it, the artist was probably renewing his earlier acquaintance with portraiture, for only one other such picture is known, painted at the outset of his career.

This, a portrait of Miss Sarah Webb of Harlaston, later of Bath, was painted in London or during his stay in Plymouth in the 1780's (**91**).

These later years are likely to have been sad ones for Payne. Both George, the fourth son, and Payne's wife, Jane, died before the 1820's. Their burials are not recorded in the records of either St-Giles-in-the-Fields or Marylebone, but it is clear that they died before 1821, as the census returns for Marylebone in that year record only six members of the Payne household living in the Baker Street house. As the age groups for each of them are given in the later columns, separately for males and females, the two females in the 20-30 age group must be Harriet and Charlotte; and the four male occupants will be William (in the age group 60-70), Henry and Edward (20-30) and Frederick (15-20)–the last being just about correct as the census was taken at the beginning of the year.[67] The two eldest sons, as Payne's Will makes clear, had already left the house. William Robert was pursuing an indifferent career as an artist and Charles had married.

William Payne died in August 1830 and the burial service was held at Marylebone Parish Church on the 12th August.[68] His age is given as 70. His Will, the transcript of which is in Appendix II, more or less confirms the suspicion that the level of William Payne's earnings had declined in the last decade or so of his life.[69] It is sad to read that William Robert had borrowed large sums of money from his father which had not been repaid. As Charles and Jane Charlotte had both married—Jane Charlotte, in the 1820's, possibly to a descendant of George Stubbs, who had resided in Marylebone—and had been provided for, the remaining four children were the main beneficiaries. However, the leasehold house in Upper Baker Street had to be sold to provide legacies for these children. All were by now in their thirties, and money was provided for Harriet to continue running the house, a task which presumably devolved on her from the time of her mother's death. Of particular interest in the Will is the reference to the models–made during his Ordnance years–which he directs to be sold. In the circumstances the children could not be allowed the luxury of retaining many of Payne's drawings: the majority had to be sold to raise more money. William Payne emerges as a kind and considerate father and his legacy to William Robert, is, in the circumstances, quite touching.

As is the case with many artists of the British School, William Payne's earliest drawings show a promise which was not quite fulfilled. Perhaps the Ordnance training turned out to be an inhibiting factor and prevented him ultimately from making the kind of response to landscape that carried the greatest artists forward to a new vision. He was unable to make that imaginative leap by which Girtin brought the 18th century topographical tradition to its most complete expression in the years around 1800 and which combined the particular view of landscape with the general, to devastating effect. Nor did he seem to possess those feelings, a compound of fascination, excitement, awe and horror by which Cotman, in 1802, viewed the advance of the Industrial Revolution, and saw, as did Turner, that Man's attempt to harness the forces of nature could be incorporated into notions of the picturesque and the sublime. In his view of Aberavon in 1791 Payne seems to step back from the works of man and retreats into a more comforting vision dictated by past experience. He did not seek the inspiration of foreign travel. In his youth he could not do so. During the war with France, travel was impossible. By the time of the short-lived Peace of Amiens, in 1802, the demands of a growing family and the need to launch his eldest son on an artistic career precluded a longer voyage than the crossing to the Isle of Wight. When foreign travel again became feasible, after the war in 1815, he did not take the risk. Concerned with his teaching practice, he lost contact with that ferment of ideas which, through shared experience, informs the work of his fellow artists. In purely technical terms, however, he did strike out on a novel path which he formulated for himself in advance of his contemporaries. He is at all times a practitioner in the purest form of watercolour art and his early drawings and occasionally his small and highly skilful later watercolours have much the same impact on us that they had nearly two hundred years ago. Although he has been labelled a mannerist, the judgment is harsh and the skills he passed on to his pupils can only have been beneficial.

The importance of the West Country to William Payne's career cannot be denied. In his beautiful and striking early drawings he made an immediate response to the scenery and quality of light that are unique to the South Devon coast, and though the South of Wales later had a similar place in his affections, it was to the West Country, in spirit and in person, that he was to return again and again for inspiration.

THE ILLUSTRATIONS

Sizes are given in inches, height before width.
The medium for all drawings prior to 1791 is pen, ink and watercolour.
The remaining works are in watercolour unless otherwise stated.
Colour illustrations numbers 72-83 show the three phases of Payne's style between 1786 and 1826.

1. Looe from the West Looe Road.
$10_{3/4}$ x $14_{3/4}$; c.1783.

The town is viewed from across the West Looe river in the afternoon. The reed pen is used with great vigour on the foliage of the trees, the foreground bushes and the leaves of butterbur. The town is drawn in meticulous detail. Even at this early stage, golden tones predominate and "dragging" is used on the path, where the figure approaches his waiting horse. This is probably the earliest Payne drawing from his Plymouth period to be illustrated in this account.

Private Collection.

2. **Looking towards the Sound, Plymouth.**
16 x 22: signed and inscribed no.3 on the reverse; c.1783-5.

The winding of the Plym leads to the Sound beyond. Two figures are loading hay in the middle distance. The broken foreground is well handled and, as in the previous watercolour, the tree to the right – a feature of the topographical tradition – leads the eye to the middle distance and thence to the landscape and sea beyond.

Courtesy of The Royal Albert Memorial Museum, Exeter.

3.**Looking towards Plympton.**
16 x 22; signed; c.1783-5.

A rather more enclosed landscape than the previous example, and perhaps less successful as a composition. This is probably an example of a country house view produced for the owner. The house, which has not been identified, is framed by the trees which surround it, but the distant sea to the right of Staddon Heights is also a focal point. Payne was never at his best in drawing cows and these are somewhat out of scale, a trait also noticeable at times in the figure and animal drawings of Paul Sandby.

Courtesy of The Royal Albert Memorial Museum, Exeter.

4. St Nicholas' Island from Obelisk Hill.
Oval, 5½ x 5; signed, and signed again and dated 1786 verso.

This is one of at least four small oval or circular watercolours belonging to the years 1786-7, all noted for their delicate colouring and a neatness which does not preclude freedom of handling. The eye is led over the leaves of butterbur to the grazing horses, and from there to the trees which frame the panorama from Mt Batten to Staddon Heights, with St Nicholas' Island as a focal point.

Courtesy of Plymouth City Museum and Art Gallery.

5. View of the Eddystone Lighthouse off Plymouth Sound.
Oval, 7 x 8⅜; signed; c.1787.

Payne shows no great liking for open seas, but it would have been surprising if he had failed to record the Eddystone Lighthouse, for it was a favourite subject with marine artists at the end of the 18th century, notably the Cleveleys and J.T.Serres, though none recorded the lighthouse from so close a viewpoint. In a scene like this, Payne seeks a human interest, partly to create scale. The lighthouse depicted is Smeaton's of 1757, the lantern of which was 80 feet above high water mark. It was only removed in the 1870's when the reef it was standing on began to disintegrate. The present lighthouse is on an adjacent reef, while the lighthouse in Payne's drawing was re-erected on Plymouth Hoe.

Courtesy of Plymouth City Museum and Art Gallery.

6. **Mount Edgcumbe from Cremyll**.
7. **Plymouth from StonehouseHill.**
Both oval,18₃/₈ x 14₁/₈; both signed; c.1786-8.

Both views were favourites with Payne and appear in other versions as well as the 1790 set of hand coloured aquatints. Payne makes the towering rock formations of the left hand side a dominant feature of both scenes and though this is, on the whole, more successfully managed in the Stonehouse drawing, as the descending rocks take the eye on to the tower of St Andrew's church in the distance, the Cremyll picture provides the starker contrasts. Both pictures were once in the collection of Queen Adelaide, whose affection for Plymouth and its environs was well known.

Courtesy of Plymouth City Museum and Art Gallery.

8. **View of Stonehouse and Mount Stone from the limekiln, Stonehouse Creek.**
12 x 16⅛; signed; c.1786-8.

The full inscription reads, *View of that part of Stonehouse called Whitehall - also the Long Room, and Mount Stone in the distance taken from the Lime Kiln in Stonehouse Creek, near Plymouth dock.* This is an effective composition with sharp, clear washes to mark out the shadows on the buildings, sails etc. In places, a drier brush has been used for the gathering clouds, a device employed in at least two other watercolours from the series. Such effects of dragging are normally used by Payne in his foregrounds.

Courtesy of Christie's, London.

9 - 14. FLETE HOUSE AND ENVIRONS, SIX VIEWS.

9. **A North View of Flete House.**

10. **View of Flete House from the Shrubbery.**

11. **View taken near the Hermitage, Flete house.**

12. **View of Flete House from the Weir.**

13. **Sunset from the Park, Flete House.**

14. **View of Modbury.**

Each 13½ x 19; each signed; c.1788.

The clarity and precision of these drawings, enhanced by their virtually unfaded condition, show the artist moving away from mere topography and responding to the romanticism of the scenery surrounding Flete House. There is an obvious delight in the opportunities presented by parkland, moving water and, above all, by the wooded slopes that hang above the windings of the Erme. Indeed, Payne's skill at depicting foliage in near, middle, or far-off distance, in a chiaroscuro of subtly blended tones, is a feature of all these drawings. The compositional details show imaginative touches. The tree framing the *North View of Flete House* is removed to the far right-hand margin of the picture, bringing the house itself, under the clouds which hang over it, into sharp focus. In the *View of Modbury,* with some daring, Payne reveals the minute spire of the church in the gap between two groups of trees, whose canopies almost reach the top of the drawing. In his *View of the Park at Sunset,* the sharpness with which Payne delineates the foreground plateau, with figures resting from their labours beside gates awaiting repair, in no way distracts the eye from the broad valley that spreads beneath, nor from the hills enfolding the river, as it makes its leisurely way towards the sea. The figures, appearing in all but one of the drawings, are admirably observed, their status determined as much by the environment in which they are set, as by the tasks which occupy them.

Private Collection.

9. **A North View of Flete House.**

10. **View of Flete House from the Shrubbery.**

11. **View taken near the Hermitage, Flete House.**

12. **View of Flete House from the Weir.**

13. **Sunset from the Park, Flete House.**

14. **View of Modbury.**

15. Seaton Bridge on the way to Looe.
11½ X 15½; signed; c.1788-9.

The somewhat squat figure driving pack-horses across the bridge (still there today, though somewhat battered), the tonality and the skill of handling, indicate a date towards the end of Payne's stay in Plymouth. The foliage in the foreground to the left balances the mass of trees to the right beyond the Looe road. The tumbledown cottages are drawn with meticulous precision. The figure on the beach is pointing his telescope at the Eddystone lighthouse which can just be made out on the horizon. There is much dragging in the foreground and numerous striations which successfully blend with the texture elsewhere.

Private Collection, formerly with the Fine Art Society Ltd.

16. A View of Teignmouth and the River, taken near Newton Bushell.
12⅛ x 16⅛; signed, and inscribed verso; c.1788-9.

Payne shows ever increasing skill in his handling of receding distance as he nears the end of his Plymouth period. This scene appears contemporary with the views of Flete House (nos.9-14) and shares much of their mastery and some of the motifs found in them - the tree taken to the very top of the picture, the milkmaid balancing a pail on her head, and the careful juxtaposition of warm and cool colours in both sky and landscape. The result is a sharply observed and wholly delightful rendering of a tranquil pastoral scene now ruined by a dual-carriageway and the expansion of Newton Abbot.

Private Collection.

17. **Rural Merriment.**
Circular, 4$_{1/2}$ x 4$_{1/2}$; inscribed and dated 1786.

With its small size and swirling pen line Payne creates, with economy of means, a scene of revelry. Unusually, in drawings of this period, no particular location is indicated, and various elements are imported into the scene - inn, church and estuary - to create the composition. With this drawing, Payne initiates an interest in rural life which was to predominate in his later drawings.

Courtesy of Plymouth City Museum and Art Gallery.

18. **Puslinch House.**
11$_{1/4}$ x 15$_{1/4}$; signed; c.1787-8.

This watercolour of Puslinch House on the Yealm marks an advance in technique over the earlier views of country houses (no.3), and equals the masterly views of Flete House and Cotehele. With assured draughtsmanship, Payne takes the viewer's eye along the darker trees in the left foreground, and round to the bridge and house. Smoke, rising above the line of trees in the middle distance, billows in the directon of the wood which runs towards the estuary on the right, where a vessel's mast points upwards to the more distant bank.

Courtesy of the Plymouth City Museum and Art Gallery.

19. Sir Francis Drake's Weir at Tavistock.
11¾ x 15¼; c.1787-8.

This weir, which appears in a number of contemporary versions, including at least one in oval format, was a favourite subject with Payne, and was reworked in the 1793 tour. A venerable oak arches over the weir and the Tavy's cascading waters - a tour-de-force in which clarity is obtained by the utmost economy of means. To achieve this, Payne adopts a lower viewpoint than in the 1793 version, which enables him to dwell on his favourite butterbur motif in the foreground, and the plants encroaching on the oak, with a vigorous pen-line. A fisherman on the right waits patiently for his catch, while beyond, wooded slopes vanish into the mists.

Courtesy of Plymouth City Museum and Art Gallery

20. **Okehampton from near the Castle.**
Oval, 8 x 11½; signed; c.1787-9.

One of a number of scenes of this view produced in the 1780's. There is also a later view of 1793. The town is viewed from the south. Note the obligatory tree to the right. The riot of foliage is handled with great skill and the treatment, together with its subject matter, suggests a picture contemporary with *The Bathing Pool at Okehampton* (no. 38).

Private Collection.

21. **Near Okehampton.**
12⅛ x 16⅛; signed; c.1788-9.

This watercolour, otherwise known as *Bear Bridges, Okehampton*, is similar in handling to *Meavy and Sheeps Tor,* (see no. 37) suggesting a tour via Tavistock (see no. 19) to Okehampton at this time. Pen outlining is much in evidence and the whole picture is meticulously drawn with well-balanced areas of light and shade. Payne has responded well to the texture of the bridge's stonework with its warmer colouring offsetting the cooler tones of the fields beyond. In the distance clouds begin to mass on the edge of Dartmoor.

Courtesy of The Trustees of the British Museum.

22. View of Totness (sic),Devon,taken from the Banks of the River Dart, about a mile below the Town.

11½ x 15¾; signed, and inscribed verso;c.1789.

Unusually, for a Plymouth period drawing, late evening sunlight is depicted with purple, gamboge and golden hues, normally found in Payne's second period, predominating. The draughtsmanship is as meticulous as ever with much pen outlining on trees and foreground foliage. This is an unaffected topographical view in which Payne channels the vision of the spectator along the curves of the Dart to Camden's " little town, hanging from East to West on the side of a hill" here seen behind a screen of trees. The town's importance as an agricultural centre with a weekly cattle market is emphasised by the three cows resting beneath the tree, drawn with greater precision than in some of Payne's earlier watercolours.

By Courtesy of Sotheby's.

23. Stoke Fleming.
11⅖ x 16; signed; c.1788-9.

This watercolour in its 1793 version, from the tour of that year, is inscribed *Stoke Fleming and Mr Trig's House from Slapton Sands,* but the British Museum version has always - and wrongly - been titled *Torbay.* A number of other versions are known.The dragging, freely used in the foreground, adds sparkle and richness. The sea and the distant headland disappear into a shimmering haze while the boats and winch are sharply delineated. The rock-strewn foreground is handled with greater freedom than is usual with drawings of this period.

Courtesy of The Trustees of The British Museum.

24. **Weymouth and Portland.**
11$_{3/4}$ x 16; signed;c.1789.

This fine watercolour, no.35 of a loan Exhibition of English Watercolour Drawings, in aid of the Courtauld Institute at John Mitchell & Son in 1970/1, held its own in very distinguished company. The confident handling of the trees and foreground foliage, the cleverly grouped figures and the delicate washes on the bushes and hedgerows of the receding landscape indicate a date towards the end of Payne's period with the Ordnance Board at Plymouth. The treatment of rocks and trees should be compared with that of *Quarry on the Banks of the Plym* (no.75) and *Smugglers Cave* (no.26).

Courtesy of John Mitchell & Son, New Bond Street, London.

25. The Limekiln, Richmond Walk, Devonport.
15½ x 18; c.1789-90.

The looser handling seems to indicate a transitional drawing. The colouring clearly denotes a Plymouth period watercolour, as does the meticulous detail of the foreground vessel drawn up on the shore, but the distant glimpse of Payne's favourite ferry house, with the bridge at Stonehouse disappearing into the mist, and the perfunctory treatment of the foliage overhanging the rocks on the left, look forward to the change of style which was to follow. Richmond Walk was constructed by the Duke for the benefit of the inhabitants of Stonehouse and Dock, giving access to a beach which was to become, in the early 19th century, a favoured bathing place.

Courtesy of Plymouth City Museum and Art Gallery.

26. Smugglers' Cave, a Quarry near Plymouth.
11 x 15½; signed; c.1788-9.

A virtuoso performance, probably of the same date as *Quarry on the Banks of the Plym* (no. 75). Dragging is used, not only in the foreground, but on the rocks in the distance on the left, where the light entering the quarry softens the contours before striking the rocks that overhang the door set into them. The three figures, left of centre in the foreground, taking a break from their quarrying, and drinking from a cask, are drawn with precision and sharpness of detail. Payne was fascinated by the rock formations of the coastal scenery in the neighbourhood of Plymouth and draws them with great skill.

Courtesy of the Leger Galleries Ltd, London.

27.View across the Hamoaze from the Dockyard.
16 x 22; signed; c.1785-7.

Here the sail to the right replaces the customary tree and takes the eye past the curve of the harbour wall to the man-o'-war, preparing to sail, anchored in the Hamoaze. Two long boats seem to be rowing officers back to the vessel. It is tempting to suggest that the figure to the right gazing through his telescope with his blue coat and a lady sitting next to him, is Payne himself. The treatment of the sea suggests a date around 1786. This watercolour marks an advance in technical skill over the drawing of Looe (no.1).

Private Collection.

28. View of Mount Batten and the Entrance to the Hamoaze taken from Oreston Quay.
Oval,7 x 8₃/₈ ;signed and dated 1787 verso.

The figures on the quayside, accompanied by their faithful hound, point towards the vessels, gathering sail as they make their way towards Turnchapel or scurry towards Oreston itself. To the right by the anchored vessels there is a bustle of activity, as rowing boats are dragged on to the shore and a figure on horseback scampers up the slope. As in other drawings of the period, a sea beginning to surge and run, as a storm approaches from the west, is delineated by a series of small loops.

Courtesy of Plymouth City Museum and Art Gallery.

29. **At Mount Edgcumbe.**

7¾ x 10 ¾; c. 1787.

This is a favourite view of Payne's and one which he repeats on numerous occasions between 1787 and the 1790's (see no. 70). The composition with its various arranged elements, the timbered building to the right, the two workmen resting from their labours and the vessel gently decaying beyond have an obvious counterpart in some of the Thames-side drawings of William Anderson, though the rocks of Mount Edgcumbe and Obelisk hill beyond make their own contribution to the romanticism of the scene, which Payne bathes in the soft luminosity of a tranquil evening.

Courtesy of Plymouth City Museum and Art Gallery.

30. Plymouth Sound taken near the Battery at Mount Edgcumbe.
12 x 16; signed and inscribed; c.1786-8.

Interest is focused on the figures hauling and coiling the rope, as much as on the scene itself. The waves are handled with a surer touch than usual in work of this period. The Mount Edgcumbe Battery and the fortifications on St Nicholas' Island, seen here in the centre, with Staddon Heights beyond, were doubtless drawn by Payne as part of his Ordnance duties. Note the dragging in the foreground. Romanticism is added to the scene by the barrel and anchor by the rocks, suggesting that the figures are engaged in salvaging.

Private Collection.

Fig. No.14.
The Sound and Drake's (St Nicholas') Island from the Battery at Mount Edgcumbe.

This present day photograph confirms the accuracy of Payne's topography. Indeed, at a perfunctory glance, as the distant view dissolves into Plymouth's perennial mists, little appears to have changed. To the left, across the waters of the Barnpool, on the opposite shore, in Payne's time, the batteries of Eastern and Western King were situated, complementing the Mount Edgcumbe Fort and prompting Granville to record in 1812 that "the batteries on Eastern and Western King on the peninsula from Stonehouse...are well situated to annoy an enemy before they can reach the strait into Barnpool, when those of Mount Wise would be ready to give them a warm reception."

31. **Stonehouse Bridge and Mount Edgcumbe.**
11¼ x 15¼; signed; c.1786.

The drawing of the houses beyond the bridge is reminiscent of the handling in illustration no.1, as is the treatment of the distant boats and the water. However, this is an altogether more confident drawing, one of a series of drawings of Plymouth of similar size, sharply drawn, and providing an accurate record of Plymouth, Dock and its environs in the 1780's. Note the tower of Maker Church to the right of Edgcumbe Park with the signal station which communicated with the Mount Wise Battery. This "early warning" system was immediately linked via Mount Wise to a chain of other stations on hills to the east. By this means a message could be passed to London and back within twenty minutes, if conditions were favourable. Payne first exhibited a picture of Stonehouse at the Royal Academy in 1786 (see no. 33) but this view appears to have been a favourite of the artist's and at least two versions are in existence.

Courtesy of Plymouth City Museum and Art Gallery.

32. **Plymouth from Stonehouse Hill.**
15 x 12$_{1/2}$;signed,and inscribed verso; c.1786.

This upright view is a reworking of Queen Adelaide's oval view (no. 7) and is perhaps more effective as a composition. It was on this drawing that Payne based his hand-coloured soft ground etching of 1790 entitled "Plymouth from the Footpath over Stonehouse Hill." All the versions exploit the picturesque qualities of the scene and the figure on the right seems to be drawing our attention to Plymouth's idyllic setting, and the often unexpected glimpses of the town obtained from its various eminences.

Private collection.

33. **Stonehouse Bridge and the Old Ferry House between Plymouth and Dock.**
10½ x 15½; signed, and inscribed verso; c.1786.

In all probability this is the picture exhibited at the Royal Academy in 1786. Payne is at his most effective when he unites litoral and marine elements, and no doubt Sir Joshua Reynolds would have approved of this drawing, for he encouraged other artists, notably Nicholas Pocock, to exploit the advantages of such a fusion. Stonehouse Creek provides an ideal vehicle for Payne's skill in presenting picturesque details in which the figures carting limestone for the nearby kiln have a prominent role. The subject was to remain a favourite one with Payne although he varies the viewpoint much more than in other drawings of Plymouth and its environs.

Private Collection.

34. **Hovel near Yalmpton (sic), Devon.**
Circular,12 x12; signed; c.1786.

Basil Long, who illustrated this example in his monograph, refers to the quiet tones of this drawing and states that the dark foreground is not overdone. The colour scheme comes close to that of the circular drawing of Plympton (no. 42) and this is probably Payne's first essay in a form of the picturesque – in advance, it should be noted, of the theories of writers like Uvedale Price – which was to become so prevalent in his work later. A homely touch is provided by the bundle of sticks propped against the cottage wall. Decaying thatch is deftly suggested by the use of "dragging" on the cottage roof. A note on the reverse (presumably from an 18th century local framer) makes interesting reading, and would have provided Basil Long, if he had seen it, with a vital clue about Payne's presence in Plymouth, for it states that the drawing is to be returned to "Mr Payne, Office of the Ordnance, Dock, Plymouth".

Courtesy of the Plymouth City Museum and Art Gallery.

**35. Plymouth Dockyard taken from under the Battery at Mount Edgcumbe,
with the Royal Sovereign and Glory on the Stocks.**
13_{3/4} x 18_{1/2}; signed, and dated 1786 on the mount.

The full title, which appears on the reverse of this drawing, presents some problems. Although the Royal Sovereign was built at Plymouth Dock in 1786, the Glory was not launched until 1788, though probably its keel was laid at the earlier date. On stylistic grounds the date seems correct for this watercolour, and it is therefore to be identified with the picture exhibited at the Royal Academy in 1787, though it should be noted that the catalogue then omitted the names of the ships. The composition is a little unbalanced and a wider format, with more of the dockyard showing to the right, would have obviated the awkwardness, though as usual Payne's juxtaposition of warm and cool colours is admirable. Payne produced a number of Dockyard drawings between 1786 and 1788 (see no.36), the later drawings showing an increasing skill in the delineation of waves as well as meticulous draughtsmanship.

Courtesy of Plymouth City Museum and Art Gallery.

36. **Dock from Empacombe.**
15 7/8 x 22 1/4; signed; c.1788-9.

The whole extent of the Dockyard from the Gun Wharf to Mount Wise is set out in elaborate detail. Despite the riot of foliage, butterbur, rocks and bushes in the foreground and the fisherman and his companion pausing to gaze at the passing sloop, the eye is led immediately to the panorama of the Dockyard. Behind the windmill, in the centre of the composition, the Mount Pleasant redoubt can be seen, while at Mount Wise the fortifications and signal station opposite Obelisk Hill are conspicuous. Another version from a slightly higher viewpoint, with less foreground foliage and squatter figures, was with Christie's in 1973.

Private Collection.

37. **Meavy and Sheeps Tor.**
11 x 15; signed; c.1788-9.

The tree on the left leans back to reveal a glimpse of the Tor. The foreground bushes, centrally placed and with vigorous pen work, fall away to the left and right to reveal the figure on horseback driving his cows to the river and a faggot gatherer making his way out of the scene to the right. These figures together lead the eye to Meavy Church and from there to the hedgerows in the distance, indicated with the utmost delicacy and economy of means. The contrast of warm and cooler colours is particularly effective.

Private Collection.

38. **The Bathing Pool, Okehampton.**
12 x 16; signed; c.1787-9.

The bather, possibly a beggar, hurries away up the steps from the pool, his clothes somewhat awry. The scene is drawn with meticulous sharpness. Payne was adept at portraying moving water with the utmost economy of means and remains so throughout his career.

Courtesy of The Royal Albert Memorial Museum,Exeter.

39. **Near Plymouth.**
Watercolour with traces of varnish;
6¼ x 8⅝; c.1791.

Despite the loose handling in places, the bright colours and the treatment of the foliage indicate a watercolour from the same series as the Pengersick and Aberavon views (nos. 78, 79). Coastal scenes, drawn on a small scale, predominate in this year, and are noted for the effective grouping of their figures, and for the artist's response to the romantic elements of the seafaring life.

Courtesy of The Royal Albert Memorial Museum, Exeter.

40. **Cawsand and Penlee.**
5¼ x 6¾; signed, and dated l791.

In this drawing, together with the Aberavon of the same date, Payne has firmly moved into the style of his second period. The only reminiscence of his earlier style is in the neatness of the figure drawing. The distance is handled with great delicacy and a wash of gamboge passed over the sky to give the evening effect which Payne favours at this period. The smoke billowing up from under the cauldron by the beached boats helps to silhouette the middle distance figures. The device of counterchange can be seen in the mast to the left of the main group of figures - light against the dark trees in the background, dark against the sky.

Courtesy of The Royal Albert Memorial Museum,Exeter.

41.

41. Plympton St Maurice
5 x 6½; 1793.

42. Plympton St Maurice.
Circular, 9 x 9; signed; c.1786.

This scene, of which at least two versions exist in the 1780 period and others later, was clearly a favourite view for Payne. The 1793 watercolour shows the shift in style which begins in 1790. The fuller washes in all parts of the composition, the texturing with cloth on the middle distance trees, and the rather obtrusive dragging in the foreground, display the mannerisms for which the artist was criticised by Pyne. More attention is given to the figures, and distant hills receive only perfunctory treatment. The earlier view is more sharply observed. The tree on the left directs the eye to the church, with the castle beyond, and from there to the glimpse of water in the Plym estuary, with the cliffs above the limekiln at Crabtree. In the distant hills above Crabtree, the diluted wash of Indian ink, or possibly, even at this early stage, Payne's grey, can be seen where it is in places not quite covered by the bluish-green wash superimposed.

Courtesy of The Westcountry Studies Library and Private Collection.

42.

43.

43. Marine Barracks,Stonehouse.
5 x 6$_{1/2}$;1793.

44.. View of the Marine Barracks, Long Room, Mount Edgcumbe near Plymouth, taken from the cliffs near Stonehouse Hill.
11 x 12; signed and inscribed verso; c.1786-8.

In both watercolours Payne adopts a lower viewpoint than is usual in his drawings, to accommodate the mass of rocks to the right, which engage his interest as much as the Long Room. In the 1793 version the contour of the rocks is softened and the scene is bathed in a misty light, with a perceptible shift towards romanticism. In the earlier version the waves are stylised, as in other watercolours of the period, and a note of humour, rare in Payne drawings, is introduced by the small dog, whose paws rest over the side of the boat, as it is rowed from the shore.

Courtesy of The Westcountry Studies Library and Christie's, London.

44.

45.

46.

45. Wembury House. Lord Camden's.
5 x 6½; 1793.

46. The Ruins of Wembury House, Devon.
12 x 16⅛; signed and inscribed "Plymouth" on the
original mount; c.1789.

Payne's watercolour of Wembury House in 1793 is taken
from the same viewpoint as in the 1789 version, but is in
an altogether colder vein and notable for the obtrusive
mass of striations and texturing which replace the
meticulous pen work of the earlier drawing (now in the
Fitch Collection - see catalogue, the Fitch Collection,
published by the Leger Galleries Ltd., 1988, no. 15).In the
earlier example, which was exhibited at the Society of
Artists of Great Britain in 1790 (no.232) the reed pen is
used with great vigour throughout and plays its part in
adding form to the mass of trees which extend beyond the
pier and limekiln and envelop the ruins of Wembury
House. The massed trees are handled with great skill and
the delicate greens and blue-greens are juxtaposed with
warmer colours elsewhere. The Lord Camden referred to
in the 1793 version was the second Earl and first Marquis
Camden, who married the daughter of William Molesworth
of Wembury in 1785, by which time the house was already
in ruins. The house depicted in both drawings was finally
demolished and rebuilt on a smaller scale in 1803.

Courtesy of The Westcountry Studies Library and The
Leger Galleries,Ltd., London.

47. **Stoke Church and Mount Edgcumbe.**
6 x 6½; signed; 1793.

Part of the 1793 tour (see Appendix V) Volume I, no.29. As with many of this series, Payne is repeating a view from his Ordnance years in Plymouth (see Sotheby's sale November, 1979, lot 183). Stoke Damerel Church, where Payne and Jane Goodridge were married in 1785, is framed by the tree on the left and the cottage on the right. The style of this drawing is looser than in the majority of the scenes, and, although dragging is used on the path, the trees in front of the church are free of the texturing device so frequent elsewhere.

Courtesy of The Westcountry Studies Library.

48. **Torrington by Moonlight.**
5 x 6½; signed; 1793.

Moonlight scenes, by no means easy for an artist in watercolour, are a Payne speciality and one which he handles with great skill, influencing later artists like Sebastian Pether. Such views enable Payne to use his looser technique to great advantage, and the light of the full moon appearing momentarily in a sky of scudding clouds bathes the whole scene in a gentle light to present a dramatic picture of the town rising above Taddiport Bridge.

Courtesy of The Westcountry Studies Library.

49. **View of Mount Edgcumbe.**
15 x 22; signed and dated 1793.

This large watercolour is based on the view in the 1793 sketchbook - itself deriving from compositions of the late 1780's and achieves, despite its size, the same successful synthesis of diverse elements. However, Payne allows the larger scene to dissolve into vaporous mists, dispensing with the obtrusive striations which, in the smaller version, cover the trees surrounding Mount Edgcumbe House. There are minor variations in the disposition of the figures. Another version, presumably of the same date, in the permanent collection of the Plymouth Museum, measures no less than 31 by 41inches.

Courtesy of Birbeck Gallery, Torquay, Devon.

50. **View of Crabtree, Plymouth.**
15 x 21; signed, inscribed verso, and dated 1793.

Although the mass of rocks above the limekiln and the tree to the right are not quite balanced on the left by the foreground rock and boat putting out into foamy water, this is, on the whole, a successful large worked-up watercolour relating to the 1793 tour. The figures, possibly smugglers - for Crabtree was a favourite haunt of smugglers in the late 18th century - are well grouped, and the handling of the trees and rocks, as well as the delicacy of the distant landscape, all bathed in a golden light, mark this out as an impressive drawing of the artist's second period. Much "dragging" and many striations are used on the sand in the foreground. An evening effect is indicated by a wash of gamboge in the sky above the horizon. Scenes of this size and importance in the post 1790 period are rare. For the signature on the reverse of this drawing see fig. 13.

Private Collection.

51. **Quarry near Oxton.**
5 1/4 x 6 3/4; signed, inscribed verso,
and dated 1793.

One of the watercolours deriving from the 1793 tour. I have suggested that Payne stayed with the Rev. John Swete of Oxton House near Dawlish and this drawing seems to confirm this. The indigos have faded to a reddish brown but Payne's skill at handling foliage and moving water is still apparent.

Private Collection.

52. **Dittisham Ferry on the Dart.**
5 1/4 x 8 1/2; signed and dated 1793.

A thin film of Chinese white highlighting is used on the dark foreground rocks. Payne uses this sparingly and only on the darkened foregrounds, the first examples occurring in the 1780 period when he experiments for a time with some body colour as well. The figures here are well grouped and it is interesting to note the horse being transported across the river, where, until recently, there was a car ferry. Golden tones predominate, but it should be noted that the picture has faded.

Private Collection.

53. On the Dart.
14 x 21³/₈; c.1793.

Despite its large scale, this is, on the whole, a successful composition and the enclosed nature of the scene prevents the picture from falling away into emptiness on the lefthand side. Payne is at his best in these river scenes and he exploits to the full the romantic elements - limekilns on the banks, drovers and their pack-horses, and sailors being rowed to and from the sloops at anchor.

Courtesy of The Royal Albert Memorial Museum, Exeter.

54. View across the Hamoaze to Mount Edgcumbe.
11½ x 19; c.1796-1800.

The somewhat colder colouring suggests a date towards the end of the 18th century when other dated examples confirm a temporary abandoning of the golden tones that predominate in second period drawings. Unfaded examples like this are rare. This is a well-balanced composition suggesting detail with economy of means in which Mount Edgcumbe is seen in misty light beyond the darker cliffs which frame the view across the Hamoaze. This is a successful version, in his second style, of the Plymouth period watercolours.

Private Collection.

55. **Ruins and Estuary.**
15½ x 22¾; signed; c.1800.

Although this appears to be a view of Plymouth Sound with Drake's Island and Cawsand Bay beyond, the rest of the topographical details do not square with the environs of Plymouth and are imported into the scene for compositional reasons. However, the details are handled with Payne's usual fluidity and the figure grouping is skilful.

Courtesy of The Royal Albert Memorial Museum, Exeter.

56. **An Arched Rock on an Estuary.**
8⅛ x 11½; c.1800.

Payne produced many views like this which present a romanticised generalisation of Devon coastal scenery. The imported devices - the church on vertiginous cliffs, travellers in distant stage coaches and the natural archway - are almost clichés, but Payne manages a successful fusion of the disparate elements.

Courtesy of The Royal Albert Memorial Museum, Exeter.

57. Torrington from Taddiport Bridge.
8¼ x 12; signed, and inscribed verso; c.1800.

Payne first visited Torrington in 1793 on his way to Barnstaple, Ilfracombe and Lynton, and portrays the bridge, then, in moonlight. Views like this, with drovers crossing a bridge on their way back from market, or bringing smuggled goods in from the coast, are very much a feature of Payne's output in his second period. The looser handling of this watercolour indicates a date somewhat later than the 1793 tour, but Payne's skill at composition makes this an effective example, despite the fading that has occurred.

Courtesy of The Royal Albert Memorial Museum, Exeter.

58. Villagers near a Washing Place.
9¾ x 13¼; c.1810.

The handling of the foliage on the right is found in other Payne works after 1795, often in drawings of the Usk and Wye. In this example no particular scene is indicated. The figure drawing is skilful enough to confirm the attribution. Anything less accomplished than this - and there are a vast number of such works often appearing as Payne drawings - should be rejected as the work of Payne imitators, including his son, William Robert.

Private Collection.

59 - 61. THREE SMALL DRAWINGS.

59.

60.

61.

59. **Sidmouth.**
3 x 4 1/4; inscribed and dated 1795.

60. **Dawlish.**
3 x 4 1/4; c.1810.

61. **River Scene.**
3 3/4 x 4 3/4; inscribed verso *Payne sketch*; c.1810.

These three small drawings indicate the skill with which Payne could work with fine brushes. The Sidmouth drawing shows the town from Peak Hill in evening light with miniature boats drawn up on the beach. The second drawing, with its somewhat lurid lighting uses the device of silhouetted figures – as does the Sidmouth drawing – to indicate scale. The third drawing, a rapid and effective sketch, retains its fresh colouring unusual in Payne works of this period, for, kept in a folder, it was not subjected to light.

Private Collection.

62. **View of the Bridge at Pontypridd.**
5³/₈ x 8; c.1795.

This bridge on the river Taff was noted for its soaring arch, its unusual span, and the three circular holes at each end, placed there by its empirical stonemason builder to avoid the collapses that had occurred earlier. The bridge had already attracted the attention of antiquarian travellers and artists. Indeed, Richard Wilson, in the 1770's, and Rooker, in 1792, both produced notable pictures of the bridge. Payne follows neither Wilson's awe in face of crag and torrent, nor Rooker's luxuriant pastoral, but, with the practiced eye of the engineer draughtsman, concentrates on its dramatic structure, responding in the way that Thomas Rees was to do later in 1815, when he described the bridge rising "like a rainbow" from its banks.

Courtesy of Plymouth City Museum and Art Gallery.

63. **Pontypridd.**
11³/₄ x 16; signed; c.1795.

Although this is a more conventional rendering of the scene than the previous example, Payne, unlike earlier artists, chooses to tackle the bridge head-on from a bend in the river and, by masking much of the structure on the left, succeeds in emphasising its bizarre appearance. In the same way, he prefers to keep the crag on the left partially covered, and this, together with the small figures, increases the grandeur of the scenery set in a riot of cascading woodland.

Courtesy of Plymouth City Museum and Art Gallery.

64. **Saltash.**
5½ x 6⅝; signed; c.1794.

This drawing, which formed a pair with number 65, is, like its counterpart, in unfaded condition. Although the drawing is in a particularly free version of Payne's second style, the graduations of tonal values and its carefully arranged elements ensure a successful composition. Romanticism again predominates: decaying thatch and stonework, the patiently waiting horse, the figures resting on beached vessels and gazing across the Tamar, all lead the eye to the town opposite and to the ship making its way past Dock bound for the open sea.

Courtesy of Plymouth City Museum and Art Gallery.

65. **Village Church beyond a Bridge.**
5 x 6⅝; signed; c.1794.

The traditional identification of this drawing with Meavy cannot be correct, so we are left with an unidentified scene. This is a successful composition in Payne's second style in which the warm foreground colour, coupled with the red and pink of the villagers' coats and blouses, is offset by the menacing clouds above the church. Unusually, in drawings of this period, no fading has occurred, and much of Payne's normally fugitive indigo survives together with the greens and blue-greens of the foliage. The blaze of light, framed by the clouds, strikes the church, silhouetting the figures on the bridge, and then slants obliquely to the cottage, where the four figures are sharply focused. Such skilful groupings of rustics are a feature of Payne's work in this period and add much to the charm of these drawings.

Courtesy of Plymouth City Museum and Art Gallery.

66. **Weir on the Tamar.**
5 x 6½; 1793.

The shaft of light, a device employed by Payne, though never so frequently as in the drawings of his pupil Glover, illuminates the weir - probably near Gunnislake. Payne was fascinated by weirs (see no. 19) which enabled him to exploit his skill at depicting moving water. Texturing with cloth is used effectively here on the rocks and trees on the further bank. Payne was probably on his way by road to North Devon at this point of the 1793 tour via Tavistock, Lydford, Okehampton and Torrington. The Tamar was, by this time, visited by travellers in search of the picturesque and boats plied up to this point from Stonehouse or Dock.

Courtesy of The Westcountry Studies Library.

67. **The Avon Gorge.**
15 x 22; signed; c.1793-5.

Payne captures the brooding atmosphere of the Gorge in a watercolour which antedates the Bristol School drawings of Francis Danby and his followers by some twenty years. The effect is enhanced by the figures, dwarfed by the grandeur of the scene, who gaze out along the gorge and the Avon as it winds its way past wooded slopes on its way to the sea. Although other artists painted the environs of Bristol at this period, notably Nicholas Pocock, none of them manages to capture the genius loci as well as Payne does in this drawing and it was left to later artists to exploit to the full the romantic aura of the scenery.

Private Collection.

68. **Rustics conversing on the Banks of the Plym.**

69. **Near Plymouth.**
Each 5 x 6½; c. 1793-5.

The idyllic tranquillity that permeates scenes such as these should not blind us to the skill with which Payne contrasts cool and warm colours and the manner in which he selects his viewpoint to take full advantage of the picturesque opportunities presented to him. The figure grouping - more ambitious than usual - is admirable in both examples. Animated conversation is suggested by the demeanour of the villagers as they lean towards each other or gesture into the distance. The inclusion of children in the two views helps to underline the obvious affection Payne feels for these rustics and their lives.

Private Collection.

**70. Part of Mount Edgcumbe and a View
of the Harbour.**

71. View on the Wye.
Both oil on card, laid on panel; circular,11 x 11; inscribed,
signed, and dated 27th November, 1797, verso.

These two paintings are, together with no.80, the earliest landscapes in oil so far traced. Here Payne adopts the circular format normally confined to his first period. Almost consciously he reverts to the style of his earlier drawings in the Plymouth example which should be compared with illustration no.29, while the Wye view is firmly anchored in his second period. Thus, the Plymouth view is a factual and literal representation of a favourite scene, whilst its pair, with its arranged elements, owes more to 18th century theories of the picturesque.

Courtesy of J. Collins & Son, Bideford, North Devon.

72. **Pentillie Castle on the Tamar.**
11½ x 15½;c.1787-8.

Pentillie Castle, a mansion rather than a castle, provided Payne, in its romantic setting above the wooded slopes of the Tamar, with much material in the 1786-8 period, as well as for the Middiman prints after Payne. Late 18th and early 19th century travellers noted that the river bank opposite the castle, on the Devon side, low and with but little wood, formed an effective contrast to the greater beauties of the Cornish bank, a feature exploited here by Payne,who omits his customary figures to enhance a solitude which is only broken by the vessel turning sharply to the right along the windings of the river. The tower behind the castle is on the summit of an eminence known as Mount Ararat, which had romantic connotations, for in a vault beneath the tower lay the remains of Sir James Tillie, noted for his vainness and eccentricity, though the story that his body was placed here before a table, set in convivial fashion, is now discounted.

Courtesy of Plymouth City Museum and Art Gallery.

73. A Slate Quarry on Dartmoor.
74. A Stone and Marble Quarry, near Plymouth.
Both 8 x 15; both signed; c.1787-8.

A comparison with illustration no. 37 shows that the location of the first watercolour is near Meavy. Payne was fascinated by quarries and their stone cutters during his stay in Plymouth, and produced a number of related drawings, culminating in his masterly *Quarry on the Banks of the Plym* (no. 75). In these two examples there is less riot of activity, and in the Meavy drawing Payne is as interested in the surrounding scenery as he is in the quarry itself. Nonetheless, the figures in each case are a focal point, as they break and cut the stone, and load it into the panniers, or stack the slates in readiness. Both pictures were exhibited at the Royal Academy in 1788, and presumably passed into the collection of Richard Colt Hoare of Stourhead at that date. They show a spectacular advance in technique, the Meavy example displaying mastery in all its details - figures, quarry, waterfall, and distant landscape - only equalled by the striking Weymouth and Portland watercolour of 1789 (no.24).

Courtesy of The Hoare Collection, Stourhead, The National Trust.

74. A Stone and Marble Quarry, near Plymouth.

Courtesy of The Hoare Collection, Stourhead, The National Trust.

75. **Quarry on the Banks of the Plym.**
10½, x 15½; signed; c.1788-9.

A pencilled note on the original backing identifies this as the picture exhibited at the Royal Academy in 1789, and praised by Sir Joshua Reynolds. The composition is masterly and Payne handles foliage, rocks, buildings and figures with equal skill and virtuosity. There is a bustle of activity on the rock face and approaching the quarry itself, and the figures are dwarfed by the scale of the rocks. The colouring is comparable with *Smugglers' Cave, a quarry near Plymouth* (possibly the same quarry) (no.26) and *Seaton Bridge on the way to Looe* (no.15).

Private Collection.

76. **Near Looe, Cornwall.**
$5_{1/8}$ x $6_{5/8}$ signed; c.1792-3.

A dramatic coastal view with a rough sea running, the figures on the beach directing what is perhaps a lifeboat back from the sailing vessel, in danger in the distance. Alternatively, the figures may represent Payne's ubiquitous smugglers. Stormy scenes such as this are uncommon and usually confined to the beginning of Payne's second period. Comparisons with Ibbetson and even Peter La Cave can be made.

Courtesy of The Royal Albert Memorial Museum, Exeter.

77. Port Wrinkle in Whitsand Bay.
5 x 6½; signed; c.1792-3.

Payne would have visited Port Wrinkle in the course of his Ordance duties and Whitsand Bay remains a favourite area throughout his life. The loose and vigorous handling of the sea and the breaking storm suggest a slightly later date than the examples of his second period hitherto illustrated. The handling here should be compared with that of Julius Caesar Ibbetson's shipwreck scene (no.98).

Courtesy of The Royal Albert Memorial Museum, Exeter.

78. **Pengersick Castle.**
5 x 6$\frac{1}{2}$; signed,and dated 1791 on the original backing.

This seems to be the furthest point west reached by Payne in his peregrinations. The castle stands above Praa Sands, scene of many a shipwreck. The combination of a ruined Tudor castle, and the close proximity of Prussia Cove, a notorious haunt of smugglers, would have appealed to the artist. The drawing is transitional, for despite the loosening of technique, which was to become habitual over the succeeding years, Payne draws the castle's surviving tower with some precision, and his treatment of foreground vegetation surrounding the rock to the right is less perfunctory than later. The absence of indigo and a sky effect that echoes many of the earlier drawings ensures that this scene retains its pristine sparkle and freshness.

Private Collection.

79. Distant View of the Works at Aberavon.
5 x 6⅝; signed, and dated 1791.

The treatment of the sky and the pen outlining on the sails of the boats are all reminiscent of Payne's first period. The looser handling of the sea and the distant landscape are firmly within the style of his second period. Payne is more interested in the figures and boats than in the Aberavon Copper Works, the smoke of which is included merely for its picturesque qualities. The vessels may well be those plying between Neath and Ilfracombe, which carried copper ore to Neath from Morwhellham on the Tamar and elsewhere, destined for Aberavon and returning to Devon with coal and smelted copper for the copper-bottoming of men-o'-war under construction at Dock.

Courtesy The Royal Albert Memorial Museum, Exeter.

80. A Cottage by a Woodland Path.
Oil on panel; 10¼ x 14½; signed and dated 1797.

The sparkling quality of this painting makes it a matter of regret that Payne did not produce more works in oil. Indeed, the characteristics of Payne's second period lend themselves well to the medium, with an added sharpness in foreground and middle distance. These cottage scenes, bathed in golden sunlight, offset by the cooler colours of the distant landscape, glimpsed fitfully through a screen of trees, seldom weary us with their repetitiveness, redeemed as they are by Payne's response to the picturesque elements, in which the figures are as important a factor as decaying thatch, irregular palings or crumbling stonework.

Private Collection.

81. Woodcutters by a Fire in a Winter Landscape.
6¾ x 9½; c.1800.

Winter scenes are rare in Payne's output, but when they occur are of notable virtuosity. The "romantic" elements are clear. Woodcutters gather by a fire which adds the only suggestion of warmth to an otherwise bleak scene. The break in the clouds, soon to be overwhelmed by the approaching storm, reveals a church tower in the distance. The castle may be a reminiscence of Okehampton. Payne has portrayed the frozen river and the drifting snow with skilful economy to make this one of the most impressive watercolours of his second period.

Private Collection.

82. Figures in a Landscape.
Bodycolour on buff paper; $8_{1/2}$ x $11_{3/4}$; signed and dated 1825.

In these late drawings, Payne reverts to the practice of his earliest period and reintroduces pen outlining in the foliage of his trees, though with much more economy. Bodycolour is used throughout and the buff paper is allowed to play its part in the tonal contrasts. The figures, as is often the case in drawings of this period, have more sharply delineated features, again echoing Payne's style in the 1780's.

Courtesy of The Bradford Art Galleries and Museums; Cartwright Hall.

83. Near Barnstaple.
Watercolour and bodycolour on cream paper; 5½ x 7¼; signed, and inscribed and dated 1826 verso.

Third period drawings such as this are painted in bright, almost lurid colours with rich sky effects often denoting evening light. The admixture of Chinese white has ensured that these late drawings remain in better condition, their colouring intact, than the general run of second period watercolours. In 1826, Payne returned to North Devon, which he first visited on the 1793 tour, and he responds with much the same enthusiasm, depicting fishermen, boats, anchors and coastal limekilns with an affection that has not waned with the passing of the years.

Courtesy of The Heather Newman Gallery. (Photograph courtesy of Bearne's, Torquay).

84.

84. **Barnstaple.**

85. **Whitsand Bay.**
Sepia wash; each 6³/₄ x 9¹/₂; each signed; c.1826.

These two views from a series of sketches by Payne, one dated 1826, indicate his normal practice in recording scenes for worked-up watercolours. The handling of both the examples is loose, but skilful. Sepia drawings require carefully graded washes and Payne was clearly adept in this technique. The Barnstaple drawing provided the inspiration for the bodycolour version of the same scene (no. 83) although there are minor differences.

Courtesy of The Royal Albert Memorial
Museum, Exeter.

85.

86. **The Tiber, Rome.**
5⅞ x 8¼; c.1819.

One of the pictures deriving from Payne's commission from John Trower (see page 28). This picture, however, was probably done for Payne's own pleasure. Its heightened colouring, notably on the figure drawing in the middle distance beneath the ruins, marks this as a transitional picture leading to Payne's third phase of bodycolour drawings.

Private Collection.

87. **The Alban Lake: View of Palazzolo.**
16 x 21¾; c.1819.

The tonal range is more subdued than is usual in the drawings relating to the Trower Commission. This is partly due to the nature of the site itself, with its grey-green volcanic stone, but it is also likely that Payne was aware of Cozens' earlier views of the Alban Lake, which are invested with an austerity appropriate to an area which contained within it the ancient city of Alba Longa, precursor of Rome. Something of this austerity is apparent in Payne's view, although, unlike Cozens, he had not experienced at first hand the romantic aura of the place. However, the traditional, if false, identification of the monastery of Palazzolo with Ascanius' foundation might well have appealed to the artist.

Courtesy of Bradford Art Galleries and Museums; Cartwright Hall.

88.

89.

88. View of Mount Soracte from Civita Castellana.

89. View of Castella Madamma on the Banks of the Anio.
Each 10 x 15½ approx; both signed, inscribed and dated 1818.

These two views painted for John Trower in 1818 are part of a commission of twenty or more drawings, worked up from Trower's sketches and incorporating a higher range of colour than earlier drawings. They are notable for the assured touch in the handling of their distances, anticipated in the early drawing of Weymouth and Portland (see no.24). With their elaborate foregrounds these are impressive finished drawings in which Payne shows that he can cope with mountains if they are relegated to a safe distance.

Courtesy of Christie's, London.

90. **View on the Wye.**
Oil on canvas; 43 x 65 1/4; c.1809-10.

Eight oils of similar dimensions were exhibited in Payne's lifetime, the subjects of which were drawn from Cornwall, Devon, Wales and the Lake District, and this picture was exhibited at the British Institution in 1810. This oil is a reworking of one of his favourite scenes, first visited in either 1791 or 1793, and in both style and subject matter is closely analagous to the watercolours. Payne was clearly an accomplished artist in oils, first using the medium for landscape in the 1790' s, preferring then a smaller scale more closely allied to the watercolours, but returning to the medium and working on a larger scale from 1809.

Courtesy of The Royal Albert Memorial Museum, Exeter.

91. **Portrait of Sarah Webb.**
Oil on canvas; 30 x 25; c.1786-8.

This is the only known portrait in oils relating to William Payne's Plymouth period, though in all probability it was painted in London during one of Payne's return visits to the capital or at the end of his tour of duty in Plymouth .

Courtesy of The Victoria Art Gallery, Bath.

92.

93.

92. Stonehouse from the Limekiln.

**93. View of the Bridge and Ferry House
at Stonehouse.**
Each 7 x 10; c.1790.

Payne produced two sets of hand-coloured etchings, one in 1792 and this earlier series in 1790. Surviving uncoloured versions show a perfunctory etched line, giving no indication of the finished product. The process was used for the rapid duplication of a number of favourite scenes in the Plymouth area, and in colouring and style the 1790 etchings belong firmly to his Ordnance years, while the later set reflects the style of his second period. The first scene, albeit from a closer viewpoint, should be compared with the watercolour in illustration no.8 and the second reproduces the view of the Bridge and Ferry House exhibited at the Royal Academy in 1786 (no. 33), a scene reworked again in the 1793 tour.

Courtesy of Plymouth City Museum and Art Gallery.

94. The Town of Dock, Mount Wise and Mount Pleasant Redoubts; Stoke Village and Church, Stonehouse Bridge and Creek;from the Amphitheatre, Mount Edgecombe (sic).
Hand-coloured etching;11 x 15; inscribed verso,and dated 1792.

One of a set of four soft-ground etchings, hand coloured by Payne and issued from 2, Thornhaugh Street in 1792. Complete sets of the four etchings are rare and their titles were unknown to the compiler of the 1937 Plymouth catalogue. Recently a set of the four, now in a private collection, was with W.E.Fox Smith of 53, Southside Street, The Barbican, Plymouth, and the titles of the remaining three were as follows:

Mount Edgecombe, the Island & Penlee Point from the East.
The Mew Stone & Sound from the Terrace, Mount Edgecombe.
The Royal Dockyard, Mutton Cove & Passage from Mount Edgecombe.

Private Collection.

95. **On the Usk.**
Aquatint, hand-coloured; 4_{3/4} x 7;
signed,and inscribed verso; c.1795.

A drawing relating to this print, catalogued as Nicholson, though almost certainly by Payne, as there were similarities in the treatment of the foliage, was with Sotheby's in November, 1986. The print is surrounded by Payne's characteristic lined wash and is inscribed in his hand on the reverse.

Private Collection.

96. **View near Plymouth.**
Aquatint, hand-coloured; 5_{1/4} x 6_{3/4}; inscribed on the mount; c.1800.

Another characteristic print relating to the early years of Payne's second period. Payne probably worked on these aquatints at Thornhaugh Street and returned them, completed, to the printer, who was probably John P. Thompson, of Great Newport Street.The firm traded initially as Darling and Thompson but by 1803 had formed an association with T. Simpson of St. Paul's.

Private Collection.

97.

97. Terence Hewitt Williams. River Landscape with Gipsies.
Circular, 11$_{7/8}$ x 11$_{7/8}$; Signed; c.1800.

Courtesy of Plymouth City Museum and Art Gallery.

98. Julius Caesar Ibbetson. Rescuing Shipwrecked Mariners.
Sepia and grey washes; 6$_{3/4}$ x 8$_{7/8}$; c.1795.

Private Collection.

99. J.H.Harding. **Landscape: Sowing and Harrowing.**
Watercolour; 8$_{1/4}$ x 9$_{1/2}$; signed and dated 1795.

Courtesy of The Board of Trustees of the Victoria and Albert Museum.

98.

99.

100. John Glover. On the River Lledr, North Wales.
11⅝ x 16¼; inscribed with title on the old mount; c.1800.

Courtesy of Spink and Son Ltd.

101. Francis Nicholson. The Dropping Well, Knaresborough.
11¾ x16¾; signed; c.1790.

Courtesy of the Trustees of the British Museum.

102. Francis Nicholson. Scarborough.
Watercolour, with traces of etched outline; 11¾ x16⅜; c.1790.

Courtesy of Christie's, London.

100.

101.

102.

103 - 105. DRAWINGS OF DISPUTED ATTRIBUTION

103.

103. **Scarborough from the South.**

Pen, ink and watercolour; 11 5/8 x 16 1/8; c.1790.

Courtesy of The Board of Trustees of the Victoria and Albert Museum.

104. **St Paul's Cathedral from Westminster Bridge.**

Pen, ink and watercolour; 11 1/4 x 16 5/8; c.1790.

Courtesy of The Board of Trustees of the Victoria and Albert Museum.

105. **St Paul's Cathedral from below London Bridge.**

Pen, ink and watercolour; 12 x 16 5/8; c.1790.

Courtesy of The Board of Trustees of the Victoria and Albert Museum.

104.

105.

NOTES ON THE INTRODUCTION AND THE CHAPTERS

1. Thomas Sandby (1723-1798) and Paul Sandby (1731-1809). Both joined the Board of Ordnance Drawing Room in the Tower of London. Thomas' royal connections were with the Dukes of Cumberland and Gloucester and also with King George III. Paul, often called the "Father of English Watercolour", though the title is somewhat anomalous, became, with his brother, a founder member of the Royal Academy and enjoyed Royal approval and patronage as a result. Both figure elsewhere in this monograph.

2. The Rev. William Gilpin (1724-1804), outlined his theory fully in 1782. The work was *Observations on the River Wye, and several parts of South Wales etc, relative chiefly to Picturesque Beauty.* William Gilpin was an amateur artist, who became Vicar of Boldre in the New Forest in 1770. The distinction between the sublime, the beautiful and the picturesque was elaborated further as the 18th century progressed.

3. Dr Thomas Monro (1759-1833), physician to Bethlem Hospital, and an amateur artist, encouraged promising young artists to copy works by Cozens, Hearne, etc., at his home, 8, Adelphi Terrace. John Robert Cozens (1752-1797), "the greatest genius that ever touched landscape", according to John Constable, was placed in the care of Dr Thomas Monro, in 1793, when he became insane.

4. S. Middiman published engravings after various artists, including Payne, Warwick Smith, Wheatley, and others in his *Select Views in Great Britain* in 1783-1787, 1788, etc.

5. John Glover (1767-1849), Payne's only recorded professional pupil, received instruction from Payne prior to 1794, according to Farington's Diary for 30th December, 1794. On Farington, see note 23.

6. William Henry Pyne (1769-1843), was a drawing master, artist and critic. The passage referred to comes from *The Somerset House Gazette and Literary Museum*, 1824, I, p.162. See Martin Hardie, *Watercolour Painting in Britain*, (1968) Vol.III p.237. Pyne probably resented Payne's success as a drawing master.

7. Richard Redgrave, R.A. and Samuel Redgrave, *A Century of Painters of the English School*, (1866). Samuel Redgrave, *A Dictionary of Artists of the English School*, (1874). J.L.Roget, *A History of the Old Water Colour Society*, (1891).

8. W.H.Pyne, *Library of the Fine Arts*, II, 1831, p.364. See Martin Hardie,

op.cit. Vol.III, p.238.

9. Payne's addresses as recorded in Exhibition Catalogues are as follows:

1776	Park Street, Grosvenor Square.
1786	Plymouth, or at No.90, Tottenham Court Road.
1787	Dock, Plymouth.
1788	Plymouth, or at Mr Plaw's, No.9 Terrace, Tottenham Court Road.
1789	Plymouth, or at No.23, Soho Square.
1790	(2) Thornhaugh Street, Bedford Square.
1809	10, North Crescent, Bedford Square.
1810-1827	49, Upper Baker Street.

10. Record of Marriage Licences, Vicar General's Office, Westminster. Parish records, St James's, Picadilly – Westminster Reference Library, Buckingham Palace Road.

11. Burwash Parish Records, East Sussex, County Records Office, Lewes. See also Appendix I.

12. W. Maitland, *The History and Survey of London*, 1739, 1756, 1760, 1772. This figure is for 1730 and could therefore be a conservative estimate for the 1760 period.

13. The coal factors acted as intermediaries between the coal merchants and undertakers (the publicans) over the question of labour. The coal heavers transferred the coal from the Newcastle boats to barges. William Payne senior's contacts with the publicans would have facilitated the arrangement. On the coal trade in London, see Raymond Smith, *Sea Coal for London*, Longmans, (1961).

14. Greenwich Rate Books, Greenwich Local History Archives, Mycenae Road. The rate appears under the section headed Church Fields (next to the Royal Hospital and opposite the Isle of Dogs). The rent was £45 giving a poor rate of £2 12s 6d and a highway rate of 7s 6d.

15. The references to 18th century London in this section owe much to the standard book on the subject:- M. Dorothy George, *London Life in the 18th Century*, (1925, reprinted 1930, 1965, 1966).

16. Westminster Reference Library, Buckingham Palace Road, the Rate Books for St George's, Hanover Square.

17. *New Complete Guide to London* and Kent's *London Directory*, 1773 on.

18. Much depends on the precise definition of "Coal Merchant". The description usually refers to merchants buying in bulk from the Factors (see above, note 13). They were known as first buyers and the number of

lighters or barges they owned varied. The larger merchants had more than fifty, while others had fewer than ten. They sold the coal on to customers who included loaders on account (some of whom owned lighters and could, in a sense, be classed as coal merchants), retailers, consumers, i.e. breweries and other large concerns, and finally, householders. It is likely that William Payne senior was a small coal merchant with fewer than ten lighters. See Raymond Smith, op.cit., p.147.

19. William Payne senior paid a poor rate of £1 10s 8d annually and a highway rate of 1s 4d, at 1s 11d and 1d in the pound respectively. This rate remains reasonably constant over the fifteen years of his residence in Park Street.

20. Westminster Rate Books. This general trend down the social scale is observable in the streets that surround Grosvenor Square.

21. *The Survey of London*, Vol. XL, part II, chapter XIV.

22. Op.cit.

23. Joseph Farington (1747-1821), topographical artist, influential in the affairs of the Royal Academy, is best known for his "Diary", which runs from 13th July, 1793 to 30th December, 1821. Farington records (1st August, 1800) that John Baptiste Melchair had told him that there were only five or six drawing masters in the late 1750's including Sandby, Bonneau and Chatelain, but that the number had grown to hundreds by 1800. The vast increase probably did not take place until the 1790's.

24. PRO (Kew). MPH 14, 15 (ex WO 34/256-7, WO 51/262-285).

25. PRO (Kew). MPH 14, 15. Payne's age is not the only one wrongly recorded. Thomas Sandby's age is given as 36 in 1781. He was, in fact, 57. (See Appendix III). The reason is probably the absence of both from the Tower - Sandby continuously on Royal Service, Payne with Sir Thomas Hyde Page in 1780 and 1781. The details could not therefore be checked personally.

26. See *A History of the Ordnance Survey*, editor W.A. Seymour (W. Dawson, London, 1980), Chapter 1. This quotes the passage about the Chief Engineer in 1683.

27. PRO (Kew) WO 34/206. The Reports run from 1778 - February 1780. For attendance at the Tower see WO 47/39.

28. PRO (Kew). MPH 14, 15. W. Allen's exercise is the last of the series for 1781.

29. See Andrew Wilton, *British Watercolours, 1750-1850*, (Phaidon, 1977), p.12.

30. Farington, 'Diary', 7th July, 1798. The date is not precisely given but was in the 1760's.

31. PRO (Kew) WO 51/247. Beatson was not unique in obtaining a Commission but the draughtsmen who did so, either in the Royal Engineers or Royal Artillery, normally served in the Tower for at least two years. The figure in this period was just under 30% and social class was, no doubt, the main consideration.

32. See Appendix III, on Draughtsmen in the Tower, 1781.

33. Sir Thomas Hyde Page (1745-1821). See *Dictionary of National Biography*. Also PRO (Kew) MPH 14, 15.

34. *Court and City Register*, 1758, Guildhall Reference Library, London.

35. See above, 1778.

36. Ll. Jewitt, *History of Plymouth* (Plymouth, 1873).

37. PRO (Kew) WO 52/12. WO 51/303.

38. As above.

39. Samuel Rowe, *The Panorama of Plymouth* (Rowe's, Plymouth, 1821).

40. A. Granville and Son, *A View of Plymouth Dock*, 1812, and Rowe, op. cit.

41. M.M. Oppenheim, *The Maritime History of Devon* (University of Exeter, 1968) pp.94-95. See also F.W. Woodward, *Plymouth Defences* (F.W. Woodward, 1990).

42. King's 44, British Library.

43. PRO (Kew) MR 1391 ex WO 78/893.

44. PRO (Kew) WO 54/217 - Ordnance Establishment, 1783-1805.

45. West Devon Record Office, Plymouth.

46. St. Giles-in-the-Fields, London, Baptismal Records.

47. Holborn Reference and Local History Library, Theobalds Road, St. Giles-in-the-Fields. Rate Books, Part II.

48. PRO (Kew) 54/217 - Ordnance Establishment 1783-1805. WO 52/37, 55.

Sturt's name is recorded with Payne's in a similar fashion.

49. PRO (Kew) 55/419 (p.203). He is recorded on the New Establishment as from April 1st, 1794.

Douglas W. Marshall, in a collated list of Tower Draughtsmen (Military Maps of the Eighteenth Century and the Tower of London Drawing Room, Imago Mundi, 32, p.40), postulates a second William Payne serving in the Tower from 1792-4, leaving then to take up a Commission in the Royal Artillery. However, the 1790 reference (see note 48) is omitted, and he assumes that his first William Payne left the Board of Ordnance in 1788.

50. One of the Blackheath drawings was with Christie's, June 4th, 1974, lot 147.

51. St. Giles-in-the-Fields, Holborn. Baptismal Records.

52. Rev. John Swete, *A Journey to North Devon*, (1789) (illustrated journal). Westcountry Studies Library, Exeter.

53. Martin Hardie, op.cit, vol. II, p.107.

54. As above, op.cit, vol. III, pp.234-5.

55. W.H. Pyne, *Library of the Fine Arts*, II, 1831, p.364:
"How many waggon-loads of woven elephant and imperial, 'ye gods' were consumed by amateur artists in the reign of King George the Third, of blessed memory, in practising the elegant art of drawing-à-la-Payne!".

56. John "Warwick" Smith (1749-1831). The soubriquet derives from his service as an artist to the Earl of Warwick. See Farington, *Diary*, December 30th, 1794.

57. On this artist see Richard Lockett, Samuel Prout, Batsford, in association with the V. & A., p.23.

58. See Algernon Graves, *R.A. Exhibitors*, for the entry on W.R. Payne. His picture was of Shanklin Chine.

59. This anecdote, though it may be apocryphal, is recorded by H. Ronald Hicks, in *Transactions of the Devon Association*, LXXV, pp.134-139: September, 1943.

60. Basil Long, *Walker's Quarterly*, January 1922, p.11.

61. St. Giles-in-the-Fields, Baptismal Records.

62. Sir Uvedale Price, *Essays on the Picturesque*, 1796.

63. For Payne's exhibited pictures at the O.W.C.S. and elsewhere see Appendix IV.

64. Rate Books, St. Giles-in-the-Fields (see above, note 47).

65. Marylebone Reference and Local History Library. Marylebone Rate Books.

66. For this and other references concerning Marylebone see Gordon Mackenzie, *Marylebone*, (Macmillan, 1972).

67. Marylebone Reference Library, Census Return 1821. Henry's age is wrongly put in the 20-30 group.

68. Greater London Record Office, Clerkenwell, Marylebone Parish Burial Records. The age given accords with the date of birth stated in the baptismal records of St James's, Picadilly (see note 10).

69. This is largely borne out by surviving Bank of England records. Up to 1822, William Payne's holdings were in 5% Navy Stock which the Bank describe as "heavily worked". Between 1822 and 1830, there are only three transactions and the account, by then in the four percents, is increased by a mere one hundred and fifty pounds. At the time of his death, William Payne's accumulated holdings amounted to £3,300, a substantial, though not excessive, sum. (Account no. 35052/2 ledger no. 5, Bank of England Corporate Services Department, Archive Section).

APPENDIX I

TRANSCRIPT OF WILLIAM PAYNE SENIOR'S WILL

This is the last Will and Testament of me, William Payne, Coal Merchant of Bridge Court Westminster. First I will that all my just debts and funeral expenses shall be first paid and I appoint ten pounds and no more to be expended on my funeral. I give to my beloved wife Eleanor Payne my leasehold house, No. 22 on Royal Hill at Greenwich and after her decease to my son, William Payne, in trust for Charles Payne, my grandson. I give and will to my son William Payne, his heirs and assigns, for ever, all my freehold, being the house, No. 18 Clarks Buildings at Greenwich in the County of Kent. I give and bequeath to, and to the use of my son William Payne, his heirs and assigns, for ever, all my interest or share in the four per cent annuities upon Trust, that either they or the survivor of them or their heirs shall pay, or cause to be paid, all the interest my said annuities may produce to my beloved wife Eleanor Payne, after her decease, to my son William Payne's children to be sold and equally divided between them. I give and bequeath to my beloved wife Eleanor Payne, ten pounds, to my son's wife Jane Payne, ten pounds, to my son William Payne, ten pounds, to Francis Heaslop, ten pounds, to Mary Griffiths my niece, wife of Thomas Griffiths, ten pounds. I give and bequeath to my four sisters, ten pounds apiece - Elizabeth Wakeling, wife of Thomas Wakeling of Rye in Sussex, Mary Peece, wife of William Peece of Hawkshurst in Kent, Anne Hiland, wife of Thomas Hiland of Burwash in Sussex, Sarah Haiszelden, wife of Benjamin Haiszelden of Burwash in Sussex. I will and order the several legacies shall be paid within six months after my decease. I give my watch to my grandson William Payne and as to all the Rest, Residue and Remainder of my money book debts, barges and coals, household goods, plate, wearing apparel, likewise all securities for money I give and bequeath to my beloved wife Eleanor Payne and to my son William Payne, equally to be divided between them, and last, I make, constitute and appoint my son William Payne and Francis Heaslop, executors of this my will and testament. I declare this to be my last will and testament, in writing whereof I have set my hand and seal this thirteenth day of June in the year of our Lord one thousand seven hundred and ninety four - W. Payne - signed, sealed, published and declared by the above named William Payne to be his last will and testament, in the presence of us who have hereunto subscribed our names as witnesses in the presence of the Testator and of each other. I give up to Thomas Griffiths, apothecary, the Bond of twenty pounds, which he borrowed of me. - Wm. Turner, No. 1 Bridge Court, Westminster, Geo. Cotter, No. 4 Bridge Court, Westminster, William Hatton, Bridge Street, Westminster. This Will was proved at London, the nineteenth day of August in the year of our Lord one thousand seven hundred and ninety four, before the Worshipful George Harris, Doctor of Laws, surrogate of the Right Honourable Sir William Wynne Knight, also Doctor of Laws, Master Keeper or Commissary of the prerogative Court of Canterbury, lawfully constituted by the oaths of William Payne, the son of the deceased, and Francis Heaslop, the executors named in the said will, to whom administration of all and singular, the goods and chattels and credits of the said deceased was granted, having first been sworn duly to administer.

APPENDIX II

WILLIAM PAYNE'S WILL

I, William Payne of Upper Baker Street in the Parish of Marylebone in the county of Middlesex, artist, do make this my last Will and Testament in manner and form following, that is to say I direct all my just debts and funeral expenses be paid as soon as convenient after my decease. My eldest son William Robert who was very handsomely and permanently provided for and who at different periods borrowed and obtained from me sums of money to a very great amount and remains my debtor, I however forgive him his debts to me and bequeath to him the sum of one hundred pounds. To my second son Charles already provided for and to his wife Charlotte I give to both the sum of ten pounds. To my daughter Jane Charlotte married and provided for and to her husband William Stubbs Esq. I likewise give to each the sum of ten pounds for some little token of remembrance. My painting and drawing materials, prints, books of prints and others in pencil, sepia etc I give to my son Henry desiring that my son Edward may have such share of them as may be useful to him and a few also to my son Frederick if he wish it. I give to each of my sons Edward and Frederick the chests of drawers they have in use, tables, wash hand stands, couches, bedding and bed linen. I give all my wearing apparel to Frederick. I give to my eldest daughter all the spoons and plate that I may be possessed of also the Globe (?), my watch, my couch bedding, and bed linen and my household linen to be given to her as soon as it may be spared. My allowance to Harriet quarterly I desire may be retained during the space of one year after my decease. I direct that my three sons Henry, Edward and Frederick be allowed to remain one year in my house which I now occupy and that they may, showing strict regard to economy, take for their maintenance during that period so much of my income or property as may be sufficient. To each of my two sons Henry and Edward I give six of my drawings and I direct that all my oil paintings and watercolour drawings framed and unframed, also my models be sold or disposed of to the best advantage and their product to be equally divided among my four children, Henry, Edward, Frederick and Harriet. I direct that my leasehold house wherein I now reside be sold at the expiration of one year after my decease or sooner if my said three sons Henry, Edward and Frederick should not require to remain in it the whole of the time and the money produced by such sale to be equally divided among my said four children Henry, Edward, Frederick and Harriet or such of them as may be living at that time. I direct that my three sons Henry, Edward and Frederick may have the use of such articles of furniture and linen as they may require during the period of their remaining in my house after which time the remainder of my household furniture, excepting such articles as were purchased by or belong to Henry and Edward, I give to my daughter Harriet. My Books and Maps may be either sold or divided among my said four children Henry, Edward, Frederick and Harriet as may be most agreeable to themselves. After the payment of my just debts, funeral expenses, the expenses of proving this my will and the legacies hereby given also making a reserve for my allowance to Harriet and the amount that may be found requisite for maintaining my three sons Henry, Edward and Frederick during that time they remain in my house, I give and bequeath all my stock remaining in the new four per cent standing in my name in the Books of the Governors and Directors of the Bank of England to be equally divided among my said four children Henry, Edward, Frederick and Harriet. Should one or more of my said four children die before the execution of this my last will then I desire that all such shares, legacies etc devised to them, be equally divided among the survivors. All the remainder of my effects not hereintofore specifically bequeathed I give to my son Henry as residuary legatee of this my last Will. I hereby appoint my two sons Henry and Edward Executors of this my last Will and Testament and I revoke and make void all wills by me at any time heretofore made and declare this to be my last Will and Testament. In witness whereof I have hereunto set my hand and seal this twenty first day of May in the year of our Lord One thousand eight hundred and thirty - W. Payne. Signed, sealed, published and declared by the said William Payne the testator as and for his last Will and Testament in the presence of us John Souter of Baker Street, Sloane Street, Alexr. Hare 92 Strand Street, Wm. Holderness 94 Sloane Street. Proved at London 20th August 1830 before the Worshipful Augustus Gosling Dr of Laws and Surrogate by the oaths of Henry Payne and Edward Payne the sons and Executors to whom administration was granted being first sworn duly to administer.

APPENDIX III

LIST OF DRAFTSMEN IN THE DRAWING ROOM IN THE TOWER, JANUARY 1781

NAME	AGE	YEARS IN DRAWING ROOM		PROFICIENCY AND COMMENTS
		Years	Months	
Geo. Haines	55	37	-	
Thos. Chamberlain	37	22	9	
W. Test	37	22	9	
Henry Gilder	31	4	-	A good draughtsman, attends constantly.
Jn. Potter	37	20	-	
Francis Gould	30	20	-	
Thos. Sandby	57*	30	11	Attends His Majesty.
J. Chamberlain	36	20	-	
J. Evans	36	14	2	
J. Read	26	12	2	
Thos. Cubitt	22	4	4	
Geo. Beck	22	2	9	With Col. Dixon, Plymouth.
Jas. Hunter	22	4	1	
Wm. Wooley	22	3	11	
S. Greathean	21	4	-	
T. Peckham	22	0	4	
S. Coltman	20	5	4	
R. Dickinson	18	5	-	With Col. Dixon, Plymouth.
H. Castleman	20	5	-	
H. Johnstone	17	4	1	Improves v. well.
J. B. Wilson	16	4	9	
Jos. Gould	16	4	9	
Sam. Peason	18	4	1	
Wm. Payne	21	2	9	A good draughtsman: with Capt. Page.
Byres	21	2	11	

NAME	AGE	YEARS IN DRAWING ROOM		PROFICIENCY AND COMMENTS
		Years	Months	
Chas. Gauthey	16	2	6	
F. Lawson	17	1	4	
F. Groves	17	1	4	
Is. Swan	16	1	3	Indifferent. Attends indifferently.
Geo. Tinling	17	1	3	
A. Spicer		1	1	
Jos. Dixon	25	1	1	
C. Edridge	17	1	1	
Edw. Withe	14	1	11	
Wm. Allen	15	1	11	
Wm. Bartlett	14	1	11	Good. Attends constantly.
Wm. Hulme	23	1	1	
H. Poole	16	1	11	
Chas. Taber	15	1	11	
Robert Sturt	15	1	11	
Val. Munbee	17	1	10	
Thos. Franklin	15	1	10	
Rt. Pilkington	16	1	4	
G. Bulteel-Fisher	16	1	2	A fine draughtsman. Attends diligently.
Th. Ricketts	14	1	1	
Job Tripp	18	1	1	
J. Humphreys	16	1	1	
Alex Watson	12	1	1	
Alex Smith	12	1	1	

The Right Hon. Lord Amherst, Lieut General of His Majesty's Ordnance.

Signed Geo Haines Plan Drawing
Reuben Burrows Mathematics
Henry Gilder Perspective

*Thomas Sandby's age is wrongly given as 36, which means he would have been admitted to the Tower at the age of six! There are also a number of discrepancies between the 1780 and 1781 lists.
PRO (Kew) MPH 15

APPENDIX IV

EXHIBITED WORKS

The original spelling is retained throughout all the entries.

List* of Works exhibited by William Payne at the Society of Artists of Great Britain.

1776   Address:-Park Street, Grosvenor Square.
74.   A Landscape.

1790   Address:- Thornhaw Street, Bedford Square.
220.   View of Teingmouth, Devon.
221.   Ditto, Exmouth, ditto.
222.   Ditto of Topsham and Powderham, from Exeter Castle.
223.   View of Eddystone Lighthouse.
224.   Ditto in Devon.
225.   Ditto on the Tamar.
226.   Ditto of Yalmston, Devon.
227.   Ditto at Stoke, near Plymouth, with the opening to the Sound.
228.   Plymouth Sound, from Mount Edgecumbe.
229.   Plymouth Citadel, from Rodford Lake.
230.   View in Devon.
231.   View in Devon.
232.   Ruins of Wembury House, Devon.
233.   Oakhampton Church and Vicarage and Bear Bridge, ditto.
233.   Tablet – View of Plymouth Sound and Mount Edgecumbe.
233.   Ditto Ditto

N.B. Enquire for particulars at the Bar.

* From Algernon Graves' "Society of Artists and Free Society" (1907).

List* of Works exhibited by William Payne at the Royal Academy.

1786   (Address:-) W. Paine, Plymouth, (or at No. 90, Tottenham Court Road) NB - the name is spelt Paine in this catalogue for this date.

586.   Penny Cross Chapel, near Plymouth.
605.   View at Plymouth toward Mount Edgecomb–a light squall coming on.
606.   Stonehouse bridge and the old ferry house, between Plymouth and Dock, Devon.
607.   View taken near St. Budeaux, near Plymouth.
608.   View of the bridge and turnpike house at Western Mills, in the road from Plymouth to Saltash Passage.

1787   (Address:-) W. Payne, Dock, Plymouth
456.   A limehouse quarry at Ketley, near Plymouth, Devonshire.
457.   Yalmton Church, Devonshire.
469.   Devotion.
470.   Plymouth Dock-yard, taken from under the battery at Mount Edgcombe.

1788   (Address:- Plymouth, or at Mr Plaw's, No. 9 Terrace, Tottenham) Court Road
502.   A slate quarry on Dartmoor, Devon.
588.   A stone and marble quarry near Plymouth, Devon.

1789   (Address:- Plymouth, or at No. 23, Soho-square)
440.   Shaugh Bridge, Devonshire.
446.   A quarry upon the banks of the Plym, Devonshire.
484.   Dartmouth and Kingswear, taken in the road to the Castle, looking up the river.
552.   Dartmouth and Kingswear, taken in the road to the Castle, looking up the river.

1790   (Address:-) Thornhaugh St., Bedford Square.
506.   View of Mount Edgecombe, with the landing of their majesties, August, 1789.
574.   A cottage, with children.
602.   View of the Guildhall and Plymouth bank.
651.   View of limekilns at Crabtree, opposite to Saltram.

1821   (Address:-) 49, Upper Baker Street
51.   Fall of Terni.
373.   Waterfall in North Wales.

1822   (Same address)
130.   View near Capel Carig, Caernarvonshire.

* Taken from Basil Long and Graves' The Royal Academy Exhibitors.

*List of Works exhibited by William Payne at the British Institution

The sizes include the frames.

1809   (Address:-) 10, North Cres., Bedford Sq.
- 177.   View in Cornwall. 1ft 5ins x 1ft 8ins
- 192.   A View in Devonshire. 1ft 5ins x 1ft 8ins
- 262.   A Landscape, composition. 4ft 9ins x 6ft 7ins
- 277.   A view Near Brecon. 4ft 9ins x 6ft 7 ins

1810   (Address:-) 49, Upper Baker Street, North.
- 196.   View on the Tamar. 4ft 9ins x 6ft 7ins
- 206.   Pembroke Castle, moonlight. 9ins x 11ins
- 220.   View on the Wye. 4ft 9ins x 6ft 7ins
- 313.   In North Wales. 3ft 6ins x 2ft 8ins

1811
- 215.   Derwent Water. 1ft 7ins x 1ft 11ins
- 275.   Lodore and Burrowdale. 2ft 8ins x 3ft 5ins

1812
- 137.   In Whitesand Bay. 4ft 7ins x 6ft 5ins

1813
- 148.   View on the Tivy, Cardiganshire. 2ft 4ins x 2ft 11ins
- 152.   View in Brecknockshire. 1ft 6ins x 1ft 10ins
- 162.   Welsh Bicknor on the Wye. 2ft 4ins x 2ft 11ins

1814
- 130.   Cottage in Monmouthshire. 2ft 4ins x 2ft 11ins
- 132.   View in Carnarvonshire. 2ft 4ins x 2ft 11ins
- 135.   View between Tintern and Chepstow. 1ft 6ins x 1ft 10ins
- 143.   View near Plymouth. 1ft 6ins x 1ft 10ins

1815
- 134.   Ivy Bridge, Devon. 2ft 4ins x 3ft
- 139.   View near Breton Priory. 1ft 7ins x 1ft 11ins
- 232.   Ulswater, Lydulph's Tower, etc. 4ft 8ins x 6ft 7ins

1816
- 13.   View near Beddkellers, Carnarvonshire. 9ins x 11ins
- 15.   View near Plymouth. 9ins x 11ins
- 71.   View in N. Wales. 2ft 7ins x 3ft 8ins

1820
- 313.   View of Aber. 4ft 8ins x 6ft 2ins
- 316.   View on the South Coast of Cornwall. 4ft 8ins x 6ft 2ins

1821
- 6.   Conway Castle. 9ins x 10ins
- 9.   View in the Vale of Crucis. 10ins x 1ft
- 96.   On the Borders of Derwentwater. 1ft 1ins x 1ft 4ins
- 104.   Thames, looking towards Richmond Hill. 1ft 1ins x 1ft 4ins

- 140.   View in the Vale of Crucis. 10ins x 1ft
- 141.   An Ice-house in Middlesex. 10ins x 1ft

1822
- 276.   View of Torbay. 1ft 2ins x 1ft 4ins
- 277.   Priory Church, etc, Brecon. 1ft 2ins x 1ft 4ins
- 290.   Torrington. 1ft 1in x 1ft 4ins

1823
- 158.   Cottage in Cardiganshire. 1ft 2ins x 1ft 6ins
- 171.   View near Tintern. 1ft 1ins x 1ft 4ins

1824
- 100.   Barmouth. 1ft 6ins x 1ft 10ins
- 166.   A Water-mill in Devonshire. 1ft 6ins x 1ft 10ins

1825
- 279.   Brent Bridge, Devon. 1ft 6ins x 1ft 10ins
- 281.   Port Penryn, from the Island of Anglesea. 1ft 6ins x 1ft 10ins

1826
- 124.   View between Bangor and Caernarvon. 1ft 6ins x 1ft 10ins
- 125.   Pont-y-Pair, River Conway. 1ft 6ins x 1ft 10ins

1827
- 131.   A View of Windermere. 1ft 2ins x 1ft 4ins
- 230.   A View in Torbay. 3ft x 3ft 10ins
- 322.   View near Swansea. 10ins x 1ft

1829
- 401.   View near Plymouth. 1ft 6ins x 1ft 10ins
- 408.   View near Brent. 1ft 6ins x 1ft 10ins

1830
- 57.   View in Swansea Bay. 1ft 6ins x 1ft 10ins
- 58.   Boats with Bark on the Wye. 1ft 6ins x 1ft 10ins

*Taken from Basil Long and Graves' Exhibitors at the British Institution.

List* of Drawings exhibited by William Payne at the Society of Painters in Water-Colours ("Old Water-Colour Society", now the Royal Society of Painters in Water-Colours)

The prices and names of purchasers are taken from manuscript lists in the library of the Victoria and Albert Museum

1809   (Address:-) 10, North Crescent, Bedford Square
        21.   View near Lidford, Devon
               £42 0s 0d. Sold 23rd day to G.W. Leeds, Esq.
        65.   Fowey Harbour, Cornwall - sunrise
               £21 0s 0d Sold 18th day to Mr. Oliphant
        138.   View near Plymouth - moonlight. £21 os od
        152.   Chepstow Castle. £36 15s 0d
        213.   Vicinity of Dartmoor, Devon - evening
               £42 0s 0d. Sold 43rd day to G.W. Leeds, Esq.

1810   (Address:-) 49 Upper Baker Street
        130.   Whitsand Bay, Cornwall £4 4s 0d
               Sold first day to Mr. Saunders, 19, Buckingham Street,
               Adelphi
        229.   View in Cornwall - moonlight £4 4s 0d
               Sold first day to Mr. Sargent, Gutter Lane, Cheapside
        238.   Pomlet Mill, Plymouth £31 10s 0d
        256.   Banditti £37 16s 0d
        308.   Coast and Channel, near Plymouth £31 10s 0d

1811   Same address
        174.   Ivy Bridge, Devon, in the year 1790 £31 10s 0d
        232.   Composition, from Nature £31 10s 0d
        255.   Orestone, near Plymouth £6 6s 0d
        296.   On the Wye - moonlight £3 3s 0d Sold
        350.   Hall Down, Devonshire. Rain £3 3s 0d Sold

1812   Same address
        73.   Conway £31 10s 0d
        116.   View in Cardiganshire £31 10s 0d

List* of Works exhibited by William Payne at the Society of British Artists (now the Royal Society of British Artists)

1827   (Address:-) 49, Upper Baker Street, Regent's Park
        316.   A Waterfall in South Wales
        397.   Four subjects, Haverfordwest - Isle of Anglesea,
               distant - View in Westmorland - Trematon Castle,
               Cornwall

* all the entries come from the original catalogues.

The above list is quoted verbatim from Basil Long, *William Payne (Walker's Quarterly, January, 1922)*.

APPENDIX V

VIEWS IN DEVON

Two volumes containing water-colour drawings, each approximately 5ins x 6½ins. The majority are signed "W. Payne," and one (vol.I, no.15) is dated 1793. Exeter, Westcountry Studies Library. The original spelling on the title pages has been retained.

VOL. I

1. Haldon House
2. Mamhead
3. Powderham Castle
4. Oxton House
5. Tawstock
6. Ugbrooke
7. Stover Lodge
8. Torr Abbey from Torquay
9. Dartington
10. Heanton Court on the Taw
11. Sharpham on the Dart
12. Fleet House
13. Warleigh near Tamerton
14. Saltram
15. Maristow
16. Exeter
17. Berry Pomeroy Castle
18. Totnes Bridge
19. Wotton – Sir F. Rogers
20. Mills at Stoke on the Dart
21. Quarry at Exminster
22. Buckfastleigh Abbey
23. Brent Bridge on the Dart
24. Plympton
25. Ivy Bridge
26. Crabtree near Plymouth
27. Mount Edgecumbe
28. Marine Barracks etc. Stonehouse
29. Stoke Church and Mount Edgecumbe
30. Naval Hospital from the Tavistock Road
31. Budleigh Salterton
32. Mannadon near Plymouth
33. Greenway (Sir Walter Raleigh's)
34. Bickley from Shaugh Bridge
35. Wembury House (Lord Camden's)
36. Mavy and Sheep's Torr Dartmoor (ed: Meavy)

VOL. II

1. Government House etc. Devonport
2. Orestone
3. Plymouth Sound from Stonehouse Hill
4. Stonehouse
5. Radford House – Mr Harris
6. Pomlet Mills Catwater
7. Western Mills between Plymouth and Saltash
8. Plymouth from Stonehouse Hill
9. Butt's Head near St Budeaux
10. Belle Vue near Looe (ed: Hooe)
11. Weir on the Tamar
12. Brent Torr
13. Penny-cross Chapel
14. Torquay
15. Denham Bridge, Tavey
16. Paington Sands (Paignton)
17. Dawlish
18. Kenn Church
19. Beer near Sidmouth
20. Sir Francis Drake's Weir, Tavey
21. Puslinch near Yealmpton
22. Yealmpton
23. Sidmouth
24. Bickham House near Exeter
25. Between Sidmouth and Exmouth
26. Starcross and Exmouth
27. Quarry at Peamore
28. Exe, Topsham etc. from the Castle Exeter
29. Nuneham Mills near Boringdon
30. Seaton looking Eastward
31. Chudleigh Rocks
32. Shaugh Bridge
33. Teignmouth and Exmouth, looking Eastward
34. East Teignmouth
35. Harrow Bridge (ed: Horrabridge)
36. Brixham and Berryhead from Torwood
37. Lidford
38. Oakhampton Castle and Town from the Park
39. Dartmouth
40. Slapton Sands and the Start Point
41. Stoke-Fleming from Slapton Sands
42. Barnstaple from Sir Bouchier Wrey's
43. Perryn Harbour near Ilfracombe (ed: Berrynarbor)
44. Tapley and Appledore from the Weir
45. Coombmartin
46. Lymouth (ed: Lynmouth)
47. Ilfracomb
48. Valley of Stones
49. Torrington
50. Linton

ART GALLERIES AND MUSEUMS POSSESSING WORKS BY WILLIAM PAYNE

England

Birkenhead	The Williamson Art Gallery & Museum
Birmingham	The City Museum and Art Gallery
Bradford	The City Art Galleries and Museums; Cartwright Hall
Brighton	The Royal Pavilion Art Gallery and Museums
Cambridge	The Fitzwilliam Museum
Exeter	The Royal Albert Memorial Museum
Leeds	The City Art Gallery
London	The British Museum
London	The Victoria and Albert Museum
Manchester	The Whitworth Art Gallery
Newcastle	The Laing Art Gallery
Nottingham	The Castle Museum and Art Gallery
Oldham	The Art Gallery
Oxford	The Ashmolean Museum of Art and Archaeology
Plymouth	The City Museum and Art Gallery
Stoke on Trent	The City Museum and Art Gallery

Scotland

Aberdeen	The Art Gallery and Museums

Republic of Ireland

Dublin	The National Gallery of Ireland

Wales

Cardiff	The National Museum of Wales
Newport	The Museum and Art Gallery

U.S.A.

The Yale Center for British Art; The Paul Mellon Collection, New Haven, Connecticut

---

(N.B. This list is not necessarily exhaustive.)

SELECT BIBLIOGRAPHY

William Henry Pyne:- Somerset House Gazette and Literary Museum, 1824 (I.p.162).
Library of the Fine Arts II, 1831, p.364.
Magazine of the Fine Arts, I, 1832.

Richard and Samuel Redgrave:- A Century of Painters of the English School (London, 1866).

Samuel Regrave:- A Dictionary of Artists of the English School (London, 1874).

J.L. Roget:- History of the Old Watercolour Society (London, 1891).

Basil S. Long:- William Payne - Watercolour Painter, Walker's Quarterly, no.6, January, 1922.

Col. M.H. Grant:- A Dictionary of English Landscape Painters, 1926.

Plymouth City Museum
and Art Gallery:- William Payne Exhibition Catalogue July 29th - September 2nd, 1937.

H. Ronald Hicks:- William Payne: Transactions of the Devon Association,
September 1943, LXXV, pp.134-139.

Iolo Williams:- Early English Watercolours, 1952. (Kingsmead Reprints, Bath 1970), pp.93-4.

Martin Hardie:- Watercolour Painting in Britain (Batsford, 1968), Vol.III, pp.237-9.

Peter Hunt:- Payne's Devon (Devon Books, 1986).

The following magazines also contain articles on William Payne:-

Apollo, Vol.XXIX, 1939.
Country Life, October 18th, 1946.
Connoisseur, Vol.CLXVIII, 1968.

Index of Places and Names mentioned in the Main Text

Index of Places and Names mentioned in the Main Text